Successful Soccer

Argentina's winning goal in the 1978 World Cup final

Letts**Guide**

Successful
Soccer

Bobby Brown

WORLD OF SPORT

World of Sport is produced by
LWT for the ITV network.
This series is published in collaboration
with World of Sport by
Charles Letts & Co Ltd
London Edinburgh München & New York

First published 1980
by Charles Letts & Co Ltd
Diary House, Borough Road, London SE1 1DW

Technical Editor: John Crooke
House Editor: Liz Davies
Design: Perera
Illustrations: Sports Art Ltd
Colour photographs: All-Sport Photographic Ltd (pp 2, 11, 15, 38,
46, 47, 71) and County Press Photos (pp 34, 42, 66, 75, 79)
Black and white photographs: Chris Hinchly
Photograph of goalkeeper of 1900s, courtesy of BBC Wales
Cover shows Kevin Keegan playing for England against Denmark
(Sporting Pictures (UK) Ltd)

The author would like to thank Pauline Ferns
and Geraint Evans for their help in preparation of the
manuscript; the players and officials of Lake United FC
whose skills are displayed in the black and white photographs;
Cardiff City FC for the use of their ground for photography;
all past team members, opponents, managers, coaches, directors,
supporters, and family who have contributed to the formation
of the ideas, standards and sense of enjoyment expressed
in this book

ISBN: 0 85097 4720

Printed and bound by Charles Letts (Scotland) Ltd

Contents

The author with aspiring young players from Hull City FC

Introduction

Like most players who have come to the end of their playing careers, I would relish being able to turn the clock back and start again. One of the main reasons would be because I enjoyed every aspect of being a player. Ever since my earliest recollections – with match days the highlight of any week – the whole concept of being involved excited me. This not only refers to my professional playing days, but also stretches back into my memories of representing St. Leonard's School in Streatham as a nine year old. Looking back I am certain that I gained as much pleasure from the very occasional primary school win as when gaining promotion to Division One of the Football League.

I often wonder how my life would have developed had Association Football not been invented, for ever since I can recall I have been captivated by the game. To those people without an interest in sport it must be impossible to understand how kicking a ball can hold such a fascination, but like many of us I spent most of my spare time as a youngster in playing some form of football. Often it was on my own, playing a tennis ball against a rebound surface – making up rules as I went along, my imagination transforming me instantly from one childhood idol to another. One moment I was Tom Finney ghosting past defenders and the next John Charles heading the ball into the net for the winning goal. It was no coincidence that whenever I played out these fantasies I was always on the winning side – which added to the enjoyment.

Although a great deal of pleasure can be gained from producing a good performance, there is no doubt in my mind that victory heightens the enjoyment that is obtained from the game. In some people's eyes a strong desire to win is considered to be a character deficiency, as they feel the game should be played without attaching importance to the result. For my part, I believe that the pleasure from any game is based on the competition that an opponent provides.

Association Football produces individual contests between players and their opposite numbers, and at the same time these contests contribute to a combined team performance. It is essential, therefore, that players develop skill and understanding not only in relation to their own individual performance, but also in their contribution to the demands of team play.

This is not a book about basic techniques; I hope that those of you who are already keen will gain greater understanding to help you fulfil your potential.

In my opinion the lesson that most experienced players learn from the game is the importance of doing simple things well. It is often said that *practice makes perfect*, but this can only be true if the practice is being carried out correctly. I am more likely to agree that *practice makes permanent*. In all aspects of life we easily develop bad habits. A player who practises playing a ball against a wall will not develop well if he continually kicks it with his toe.

To reach a high standard of performance it is necessary to develop good technique in all the various contacts that are made with the ball during a match. This alone will not guarantee success, as this ability must be produced not only in a practice, but also in the competitive environment of a match. However there is no doubt that plenty of the *right* practice will only help you to improve your playing standards.

Players need to develop skill by working in a competitive situation. Technique becomes a skill when transferred to a realistic practice with opponents trying to win possession of the ball. It is only then that true development can be measured. It is relatively simple to control a ball coming towards you in the air if you are unchallenged, as you can concentrate solely on the ball and move to a comfortable position to control it. In fact often by moving forwards or backwards an identical pass can be controlled by the chest, thigh or foot (Fig. 1).

In a match the skill is to select and perform the right technique for the circumstances. Now the player has to assess not only the flight of the ball, but also the proximity of opponents, and a decision related to distance and the time available has to be made.

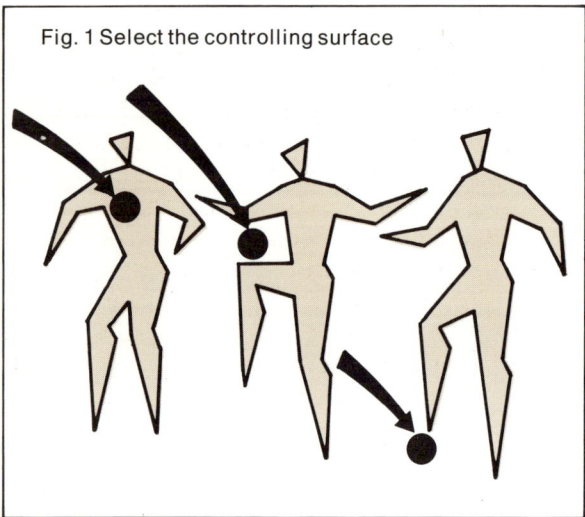

Fig. 1 Select the controlling surface

Two players, who may be able to produce equally efficient performances in practising technique may in fact be poles apart in playing ability. The fact that the game contains physical challenge will obviously affect the attitude of players in different ways. Some will respond and compete to come out on top, while others will not relish this aspect and, consequently, never do justice to their technical ability.

In my experience it has not necessarily been a higher technical ability that has made one player better than another. I believe that Association Football is about making decisions and it is those players who are able to assess situations quickly and who offer the correct response who stand out above others. Goalkeepers have to decide whether to come for a cross; defenders have to decide between marking and covering; and forwards whether to shoot or pass.

In the past players have specialised too much on a particular position or role within a team, and have been ignorant of the problems which other positions offer. The game today requires players to develop skills required of all positions and for all members of a team to be aware of both the defensive and attacking principles of play.

It has always surprised me to see a great Test Match bowler looking such a novice when it comes to batting. Basic batting technique faults are obvious and I cannot understand why they do not work to improve that technique. Whenever I have seen cricketers practise, the bowlers bowl and the batsmen pad up, I would have thought that a winter's work on batting techniques for the bowlers would have been of benefit, and who knows what hidden bowling talents the batsmen possess. I have always felt this about cricket, but it is only in recent years that I have seen the same situation occurring in Association Football.

If cricketers fall into categories of batsmen, bowlers, and all rounders, so too in the past footballers have been defenders, midfield players or forwards. Since the birth of the phrase 'total football' players are finding it increasingly necessary to develop the skills required in all positions, and an understanding of those roles within the team. Possession of the ball dictates the defensive and attacking roles of all players no matter what area of the field they find themselves in. Players should, therefore, work at all aspects of the game. I know many excellent defenders who would admit that they become almost mediocre as they come closer to their opponents' goal. As the situation becomes tighter, requiring a particular kind of composure, technique faults are forced into the open.

The same can be said of good attackers who find their defensive qualities lacking when exposed in their own defensive third of the pitch. I personally would fall into this category. I never received any advice about how to defend and any improvement in my defensive expertise was mainly due to my own observations and learning by mistakes.

This is why, like most players, I would love to turn the clock back, as I believe I was capable of being a much better player. I hope that you, on reading this book, will gain some understanding of this fabulous game and be encouraged to seek the same enjoyment that the game has given to me.

Chapter 1 Evolution of the game

Systems of play

Since the beginning of Association Football there have been few major changes in the laws of the game and yet football seems to have altered in style almost as often as fashion. If ever you see snatches of film of bygone years they are always dated by their poor quality and by the playing kit and boots worn by the players. Even if it were not for these 'give away' signs it would not be too difficult to work out the era in which the match took place.

If the laws have been fairly consistent and the game is still between two teams consisting of eleven players, what is it that has caused football to undergo such great changes? One of the major factors has been in the various ways that teams have deployed their players. This has varied considerably over the years. It has always been the top clubs or countries which have had this influence and have caused clubs playing at all levels to imitate them.

In the earliest days of Association Football very little intentional passing took place, and the player in possession of the ball tried to gain as much ground towards his opponents' goal by dribbling or kicking ahead and chasing, until he was dispossessed by an opponent. His team mates supported him close to the ball hoping to collect any loose ball through loss of control or an opponent's tackle. The game ebbed and flowed, with the ball acting as a magnet, with both teams packing around the man in possession. It was not unlike watching children today when they first have the opportunity to play the game.

If it were possible for a pioneer of the game to return to observe a present-day match I very much doubt if he would recognise the game as being the same – unless it was a match with young beginners. Attack was predominant in the players' minds and the easiest way to defend was to pack in front of the opponent with the ball. Right from the start defensive strategy was dictated by the method employed by the attacking team.

First developments

As the game developed the first tacticians began to realise the value of a player deliberately playing the ball to a colleague away from the ball, in order to transfer the attack from the main mass of defenders. It was only then that the game started to develop into the passing game that we know today. This became the most important feature in play, and today you are likely to hear the expression, 'If you can't pass you can't play! Just what this means we will discuss later.

When passing first took place it had the effect of drawing players away from the ball to find space. It not only took attackers away from the ball, but also defenders, who withdrew from the main pack to mark their opponents in an attempt to deny them time and space and to cut off and reduce passing opportunities. Reducing the numbers around the man in possession allowed the development of the skills that we know today and developed the game into a spectator sport as well as one for players. Therefore, it can be seen that the new attacking strategy prompted the defensive system to be adjusted to cope with the new problems that were posed by the attacking team.

1925 and after

Throughout the history of the game changes in attacking fashions have been counteracted by defensive organisation. This was particularly true when in 1925 the offside law was changed. Before that time it was necessary for a player to have three opponents between him and the opponents' goal line, but from 1925 this number was reduced to two. Obviously, this had a tremendous effect on game strategy and it was from this date that football as we know it today was developed. Scoring opportunities increased dramatically and the role of defenders altered. All games have certain basic principles which are accepted as being the very foundation of the game. Association Football is no exception and later we shall look at both the attacking and defensive principles of play which have been universally accepted since 1925.

9

W M formation

For many years the system of play that dominated world football was known simply as the W M formation. The reason for the name can be easily understood when the formation is seen in Fig. 2.

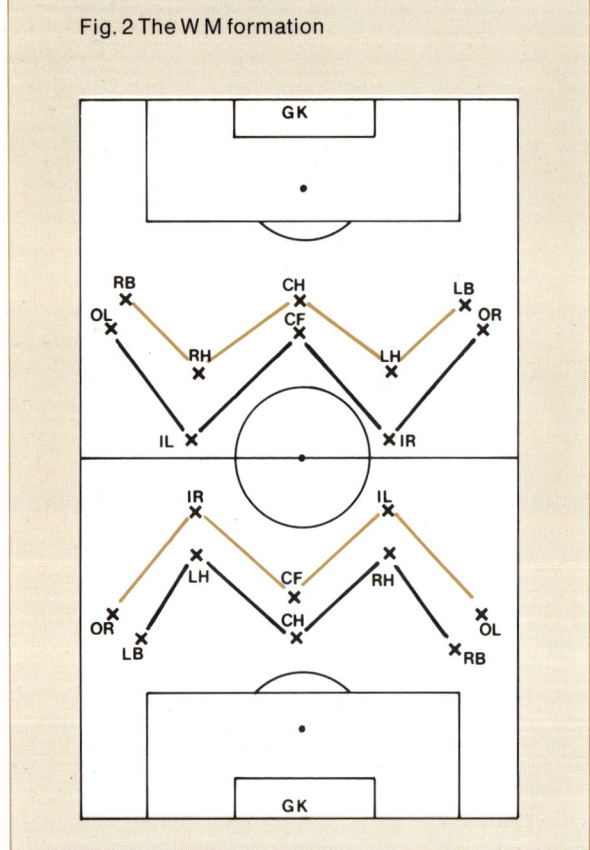

Fig. 2 The W M formation

The system provided 10 man to man contests, each player knowing clearly who his opposite number was. Eight players competed in midfield; two half backs marked the two inside forwards of the opposite team; full backs marked wingers and the centre half marked the opposing centre forward. Each player's role was simple to define and in the main the three rear defenders did not become involved in attacking play

and centre forwards and wingers were out and out attackers. Every side played with wingers who played wide. They were usually quick and were good crossers of the ball, which enabled powerful centre forwards to challenge the centre half to win the aerial battles.

The defensive organisation was straightforward with the team using the centre half as a swivel – as can be seen when play is changed from right to left (Fig. 3).

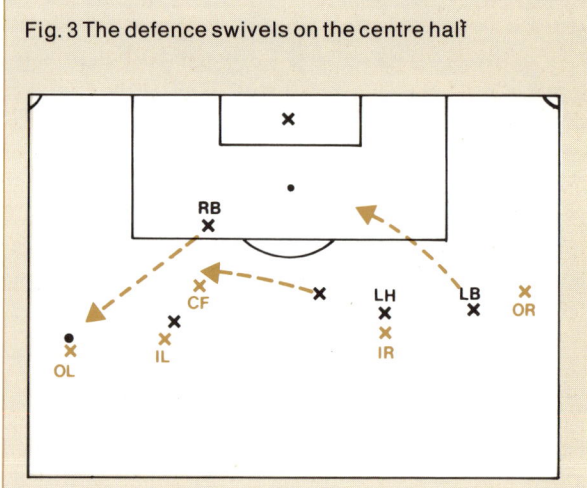

Fig. 3 The defence swivels on the centre half

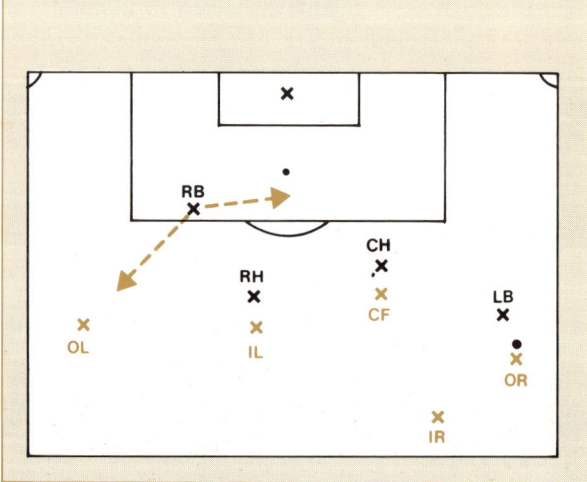

Di Stefano and Bobby Charlton, two all time greats

1953 — The Hungarian revolution

In 1953 the Hungarians came to play England at Wembley and the match has gone down in history – it provided a shock lesson which will always be remembered. The Hungarian team contained players of high technical ability who were ahead of the English players in skill. England's main downfall in their six goals to three defeat, was the system of play which the Hungarians adopted. The home team was confronted by a system that completely confused it. Instead of the accepted W M formation, the Hungarians withdrew their centre forward into midfield and pushed the two inside forwards into advanced attacking positions,

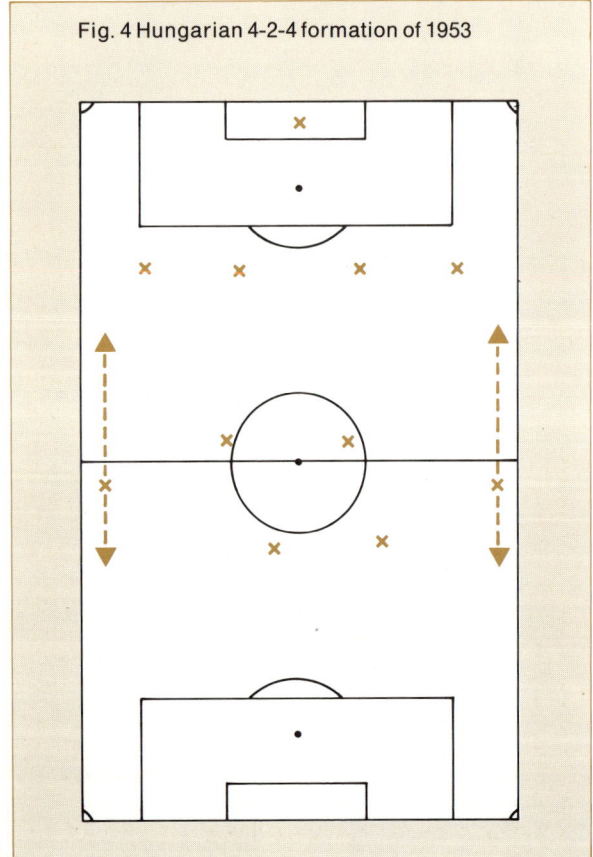

Fig. 4 Hungarian 4-2-4 formation of 1953

which caused the England players problems in trying to decide who should mark whom. The England centre half, Johnston, found that instead of the usual one centre forward, which he was accustomed to, he was now confronted by two players (Fig. 4).

The English wing halves were confused and did not know where to mark. The midfield players were drawn back into unfamiliar positions marking the extra forward, but as the responsibilities of the role were new they were often found lacking in this new challenge, providing the Hungarians with opportunities to score.

Despite the game being 11 against 11, it appeared that in all departments England were outnumbered. This was due to the high work rate that the Hungarian midfield players were prepared to undertake not only to support their attack, but also to form the first line of defence when England gained possession. Their wingers also worked hard reinforcing in midfield to produce four players across the middle when defending, and then springboarding into forward wing positions when possession was gained (and the side started to move forward to attack the opponents' goal). At the back, four players marked the three traditional English forwards and they were able to provide a covering defender in such a way that was new to the English players. The fact that there were four players instead of three in defence also meant that the full backs could be released to an extent from their W M covering role and could mark the wingers more tightly. This made it more difficult for the wingers to be found with the ball.

One aspect that was a particular feature of W M play was the long pass made from one side of midfield to find the opposite winger. This was always possible because of the swivel system which took the full back into covering positions, often leaving the winger in space. Playing four players across the back of the defence reduced this possibility, which was another factor in England's defeat.

Although it would appear that England would have held a numerical advantage in midfield, in practice this was not the case. The work load undertaken by each Hungarian was greater than that of the English players and the winger on the opposite side to the position of the ball was prepared to tuck into midfield to even out this situation.

Not only did this match provide an unexpected result, but the lesson was re-emphasised shortly afterwards in the return match, which Hungary won by seven goals to one in Budapest.

The Revie plan

The effect of these results was seen in the strategy that was adopted over the next few years by the leading clubs. Manchester City was one of the successful sides of the decade and played with the Revie plan, which was based on the Hungarian system. This was the birth of the 'deep-lying centre forward'.

To compensate for the numerical disadvantage faced by defenders, teams began to play with four defenders so that two centre halves could mark the two strikers. To provide cover in such a situation the technique of playing off one another was developed so the central defender nearer the ball marked tightly and his co-defender took up a position which provided support, and at the same time kept him in a position to challenge his own opponent should the ball be transferred to him. It is always important when marking an opponent to position yourself where you can see both the opponent and the ball at exactly the same time and be close enough to challenge should the ball be played to your opponent.

There have been several variations on the theme consisting of four back players. Usually the two central defenders selected which of the two strikers would be their main responsibility, and then jointly played a 'mark and cover' role. The general rule was to mark tightly when the ball was nearer to your opponent than to your co-defender's man, and that the marking position should be relaxed to a 'half and half' position when the situation was reversed, as can

be seen in Fig. 5. No. 4 is marking tightly because the ball is closer to his man (No. 9) than his team mate's opponent (No. 10) (Fig. 5A).

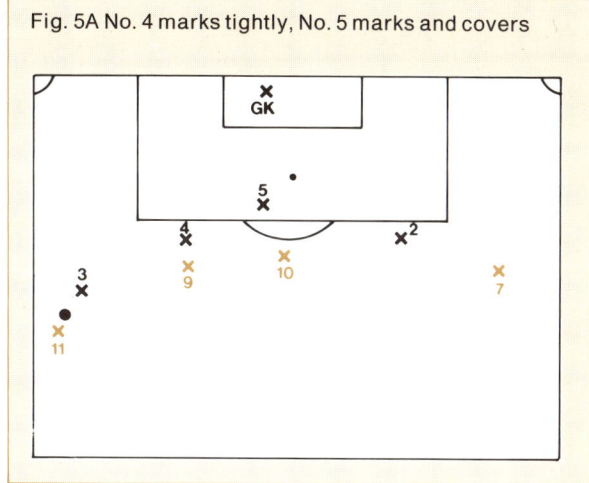

Fig. 5A No. 4 marks tightly, No. 5 marks and covers

In Fig. 5B No. 10 has the ball therefore No. 5 defender challenges and No. 4 defender goes into a half cover/half marking role.

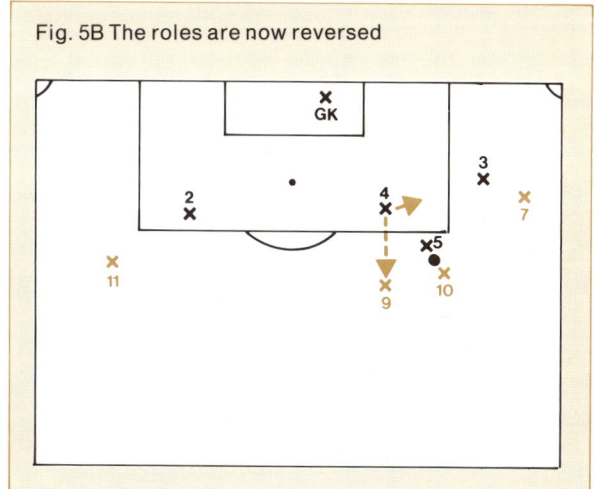

Fig. 5B The roles are now reversed

The bolt system

Continental teams often used a system which was known as the bolt system, which was so named be-

13

cause it required the full back farthest away from the ball to 'slide' across the back of the defence into a covering position. This permitted the other three defenders to mark their opponents closely. The left back has challenged the black's No. 7 and the No. 5 has marked the striker (No.10) closely as in the systems discussed previously. No. 4 is marking No. 9 tighter than before as now the right back (No. 2) has moved across into a covering position. Note the recovering run of the No. 7 (Fig. 6).

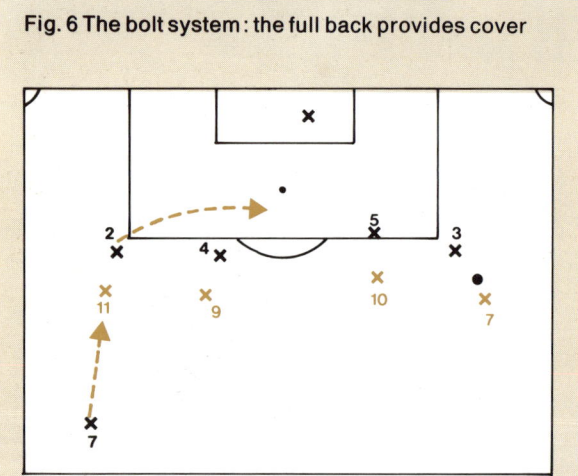

Fig. 6 The bolt system: the full back provides cover

The long distances needed to be covered by 'the bolt player' were one of the disadvantages of the system, because the defending side was vulnerable if a man to man situation was created and exploited before the 'bolt' player had time to move into the covering position. Another problem was that when the bolt player moved behind his co-defenders he neglected his marking responsibilities, and an obvious defensive weakness could be exploited if this spare man could gain possession of the ball. The defending team relied upon another member of their side to drop back to mark this danger. It was usually the responsibility of the winger to cover this situation and even if he was unable to move 'goal side' of his player, he could often

restrict the passing possibilities to the winger by merely dropping back into a deeper position.

Another variation of the system was used by some teams who employed one of the central defenders as 'the bolt' while the other central defender took on the role of marking and challenging the opponent who threatened to receive the ball. The full back farthest away from the ball relaxed his marking position and moved around to provide extra cover, but at the same time was able to challenge his opponent should play be transferred to his side of the field.

Some teams base their play on good defence and sacrifice their attacking possibilities. Italian football has often been criticised for being ultra defensive by playing four defenders marking their opponents in a man to man system, with an extra player playing behind the four defenders, with sole responsibility for providing cover (Fig. 7).

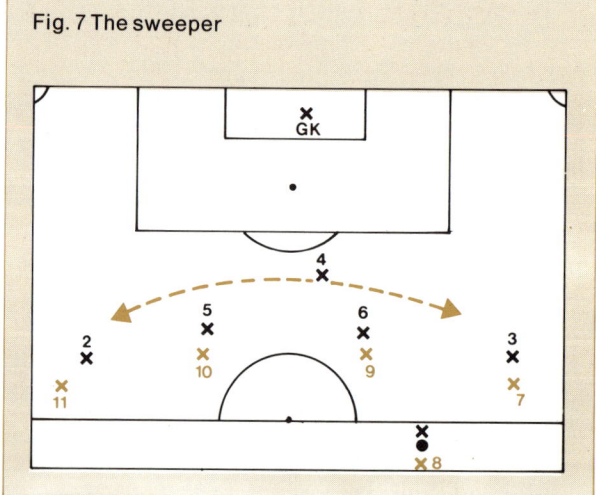

Fig. 7 The sweeper

The sweeper

This method of play was known as the 'sweeper' system with the covering player's responsibilities being the reason for its name. The sweeper literally cleans up the defence by always providing the extra man. The main quality required was to be able to 'read' the game well. Attackers tried to push a player

Ray Kennedy gives a superb demonstration of the basic skill of kicking

forward onto 'the sweeper' in order to destroy this cover and also to set one against one at the rear of the defence. Good sweepers made this difficult by moving forward, causing such attackers to be caught offside and always providing the depth that defence requires. Often defences using this style were capable of soaking up much pressure, which drew the opposition forward only to find to their cost that they were caught out by a quick break.

Modern football has seen more and more teams using four defensive players with three midfield players and three attackers. Usually one of the attackers has been used to play wide. This 4-3-3 system has required the players to be very mobile to enable forward players to find space, and midfield players both to support their attacks and form the first lines of defence.

Defensive players are continually required to increase their awareness of attacking possibilities, often to provide width to an attack – for example, when full backs combine with team mates to provide an overlap.

In the past few years many teams have played in a 4-3-3 system, whereas others have used a 4-4-2 style with the wide midfield players providing many passing opportunities when building an attack, and also pushing forward in wide positions to add to numbers of attacking players. With more and more teams using only two or three forward players, some defences have reduced their number of back defenders to three with an extra player moving forward to play in front of his rear defenders.

Coping with the systems

Systems of play have certainly had a large effect on the development of the game. Leading coaches have always explored possibilities of presenting opponents with new problems and often this has resulted in a new system of play. Perhaps you will appreciate the point by the following example. When teams have been accustomed to defending in a particular way it is always interesting to see how they cope when presented with a new problem. For example, a back four who are accustomed to the two central defenders marking the two strikers, with a full back picking up the spare attacker, would have certain decisions to make if the attackers changed their positions as shown in Fig. 8.

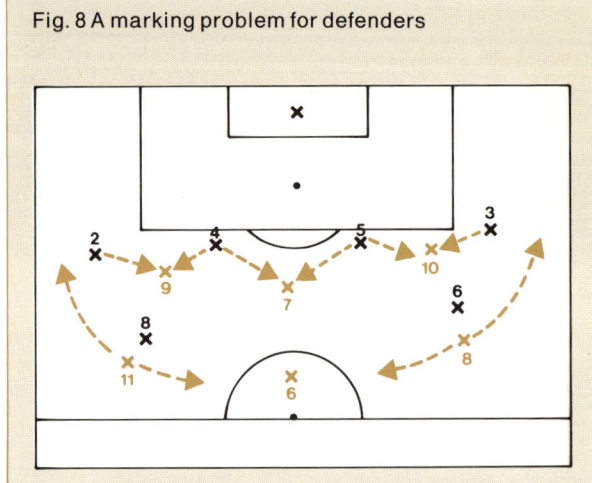

Fig. 8 A marking problem for defenders

We see that the two strikers have moved farther apart to take up positions between the central defenders and the full backs with the third attacker moving into a deep lying position forming a triangle of forward players. You can imagine the problems that have been created. If the central defenders move wider to mark the strikers, a gap is left in defence, and if one of the defenders pushes forward, then space and a man for man situation develops at the rear of the defence.

Whichever solution the defenders decide upon, it has to be implemented quickly and if the front players are mobile it will aggravate the problems of who should mark whom, for both central defenders and full backs can be drawn into positions that will make the defence vulnerable. From a defensive point of view a decision understood by all defenders has to be taken quickly and this is where experienced players are an asset to a team. The one point that should always be remembered is that no matter which system is adopted, a team always consists of 11 players. No two teams consist of exactly the same type of players and, therefore, even if two teams use the same system of play, it is most likely that they will play in different ways. This can also be dictated by the attitude of the coach responsible for the team. One coach may be defensively oriented and prevent his defenders from supporting his team in the attacking half, whereas another coach may encourage his players to do the opposite, and his tactics may include full backs overlapping, in the view that attack is the best method of defence.

The important rule that should be remembered when deciding on the system to be used is to make sure that it is based on the type and ability of the players concerned. Do not try to use a system that is not suited to the players at your disposal. At the present time it would appear that wingers are, once again, becoming a feature of the game, but it would be wrong to introduce a 'fashionable' method of play if the team involved does not have players with the necessary capabilities to carry it out.

As you have seen, Association Football has developed from simple beginnings to a game that stimulates millions of people across the world. It will be interesting to see how the game progresses in the future. That future and the development of the game lie in the hands of leading administrators and coaches. It is possible that a major change in the laws will be the basis of great alterations in football, as occurred in 1925. Whatever happens in that direction, leading coaches will constantly be presenting new ideas, and no doubt the top teams will always be the innovators, subsequently to be copied at all levels.

It's not only systems of play which change! On the left a goalkeeper of the 1900s; on the right 1980s style.

Chapter 2 Developing the individuals

Systems of play are merely methods of arranging players on the field of play, which help them to understand their responsibilities as individuals and also as members of a team. Often coaches place too much emphasis on systems, particularly at youth and junior level – no system will provide success if, for instance, the players are incapable of passing accurately. Players need to:

1   Identify and strive to acquire the qualities needed in a good player
2   Become proficient in the many techniques demanded in football
3   Understand the principles of attack and defence.

In this chapter I shall describe the qualities needed and tips for practising. The techniques and principles will be discussed in the following chapters.

Qualities of the good player

The seven factors below represent a breakdown of the demands that the game makes. Players should work to improve in each and every aspect and coaches can use the headings to plan their work.

1   Skill
2   Speed
3   Strength
4   Stamina
5   Tactical appreciation
6   Functional appreciation
7   Reaction

Skill is the most important quality for players to possess. There is nothing that gains more respect than a player's skill – not only from spectators, but also from opponents. Ability is the most valuable natural possession and it is those people who exploit their full potential who rise to the top. Players should always work to improve their level of skill. It is only skilful players who always look as if they have plenty of time. Skill can be defined as 'the ability to reach a pre-determined target with the maximum certainty, the minimum output and within the shortest time'. As far as football is concerned this statement should be qualified because it is also in relation to selection and timing, for sometimes it is not how quickly it should be done, but when, and then with appropriate speed. *Speed* is always an asset and the ability to be quick over short distances will provide the extra metre of space to exploit skill. This must be linked to change of pace, direction and movement off the mark.

During matches players are expected to withstand physical challenge, to leap high to head or catch a ball, and many other movements to which *strength* contributes to success. More mistakes are made towards the end of matches and this must be linked to the fitness of players. Fitness must be related to the activity – although a gymnast may be extremely fit, he would most likely find the varied demands of football or squash very different from his own sport. Players should, therefore, build up the *stamina* that is required for 90 minutes of football.

In addition to the physical aspects, players have to understand how their team has decided to approach the match and have a *tactical appreciation* of the overall strategy to enable players to combine into a unit. Each player has a contribution to make to the overall team play and must be fully aware of the demands of his position, whether he is a full back or goalkeeper. This *functional appreciation* requires, therefore, players to become conversant with the many demands their position makes. All players need to be able to respond quickly in any given situation. *Reaction,* or decision making, is another feature of play. Players of similar technical ability can be quite different in a match for one may read the game so much better than another.

Practising

Techniques must be practised from an early age and even experienced senior players should devote considerable time to developing and maintaining their level of ability. Practices should be set up to cover the wide range of skills that are required in the game to allow players to gain an understanding of how a ball reacts to the various contacts that are made. Unfortunately, players of all ages tend to spend their practice sessions in competitive situations, which have very little transfer value to the game.

Young players are too often capable of dictating to their team organisers how they spend their football practice. This results in either a match between teams consisting of 11 or more players or, alternatively, if an indoor facility is used, a game in restricted space with little chance for anybody to learn anything. It has not been unknown to witness a school game's period consisting of a match with 15 players a-side, purely because there are 14 players short to make two complete matches! Young footballers must be given the opportunity of making a large number of touches on the ball so that they learn by experience how a ball reacts to the various contacts. Therefore, the games lesson would have been better organised if three five-a-side games took place to give all boys the chance of touching the ball several times. In this way it is also possible to transfer coaching points to individuals as well as to groups of players.

Training sessions for more experienced players often take the form of fitness sessions followed by small-sided games in restricted areas. With a little thought and planning it is quite possible to organise an interesting session which caters for the fitness aspect as well as providing technique and skill practice, which has a high transfer value to the full game.

If you are responsible for organising practice sessions for young players, remember that it is always disappointing to see large numbers playing on one pitch when other footballs are available to be used. Organisation is very important and it is infinitely more

advantageous to the development of players, if small-sided games can be played in areas large enough for the players to find space, rather than a large group of players chasing one football. Inexperienced players always crowd the ball and it is usually only the most competitive and better players who touch the ball and even the contacts that they achieve certainly do not assist in the acquisition of skill, for the mass of other players restrict any quality of performance. In this situation it is quite an achievement to touch the ball and many of the players may play for some time without making any contact at all.

One of the most difficult tasks for those organisers of young players is to convince them of the importance of practising techniques rather than simply playing games. Sessions can always be completed by a competitive game, but many techniques and skills can also provide a competitive element or challenge throughout the training programme. Many aspects of the game, which in isolation seem uninteresting, can be presented in a manner which encourages performers to work for improvement.

In any walk of life it never does any harm to return to the real basics. Indeed, it is not uncommon for professional players attending a course designed for coaches, to gain tremendous stimulation from examining techniques in detail. Most sportsmen go through periods when, for unknown reasons, a particular feature of their play becomes unreliable. It may be a golfer whose putting has gone astray, or a tennis player whose service has become less accurate. At these times they usually return to examine the basics of the technique to discover the trouble.

Chapter 3 **Possession**

The team that can command greater possession during a match usually controls the game and, therefore, is more likely to win the contest. This is not always the case, for possession, as we all know, needs to be converted into goals. We have all had experience of matches which have been won by a team, outplayed for most of the match, accepting one of their rare chances, with the dominant side either squandering their opportunities or, worse still, not turning their possession into scoring opportunities.

Bearing this in mind, the game is based on competition for the ball and players must learn how to retain possession long enough to threaten the opponents' goal. Possession is the vital issue, for the team with the ball is the attacker with an opportunity to score, and its opponents must combine to make it difficult for the opposition to succeed and at the same time look for the opportunity to win back possession. In many cases the defending team does not have to work too hard for the deficiencies in its opponents' play often presents it with the ball through poor control or passing.

Passing

It is important that teams develop the ability to string passing sequences together to place their opponents' goal under pressure. Teams that are competent in this feature of the game gain confidence for it is without doubt one of the most important aspects of the game.

If possession is not to be lost players must combine to provide passing opportunities for the man on the ball, whether he be the goalkeeper or an outfield player. Players who do not receive support are usually dispossessed by a tackle because they have held on to the ball too long in the hope that a team mate will show for the ball, or, alternatively, they are forced into playing an optimistic pass, which has little or no chance of finding a member of their team.

Even when a team mate does find a good position to receive a pass the quality of the pass must be good enough to avoid interception and, equally, the receiv-ing player must control the ball efficiently to avoid being dispossessed by a challenging player.

Indeed, passing is not as simple as many people imagine, for in fact it is a complex combination of three techniques, and teams are required to be able to *control, pass* and *support* to enable a sequence of passes to be made. Therefore, if possession is to be exploited to the full players must become technically sound in all three roles.

Control

One of the most fundamental techniques required of players in Association Football comes under the heading of *control,* for every individual is required to receive passes and to retain possession of the ball until the decision is taken to pass to a team mate, or perhaps shoot at goal. In addition every player should try to intercept the passes of the opposition, and it is necessary to work hard on these basics from an early age, so that good habits are formed in all the various situations that require the ball to be controlled.

What do we actually mean by control? Practice situations can enable players to work at mastering football, but the target that all footballers are striving to achieve must be related to the standards that they can attain in match conditions. The ultimate is to reach a high level of performance in assessing the situation before receiving a pass, to enable the ball to be manoeuvred in the minimum time to the most advantageous position. Constant practice in receiving a variety of services can help players to develop the ability to bring footballs under control with as few touches as possible, but to achieve high standards, players must develop an understanding of how a ball reacts to contact as this is a necessary feature in acquiring this vital skill.

Developing touch

Players need to cultivate a feeling for the ball, which will help in their assessment of how hard the ball needs to be played and the type of contact that is needed to carry out the required skill. Players with a delicate feel or touch for the ball are undoubtedly the most skilful for they quickly assess situations and are able to apply the correct weight of contact to the ball.

Balance is also an essential asset from which many of the footballer's skills flow. Individuals should practise ball playing on their own, moving the ball from one foot to the other, with various parts of both feet. This will help to improve balance and mobility. At the same time it provides practice in 'dragging' the ball in all directions and builds confidence. Soon beginners will be capable of playing the ball without looking down. This assists in improving a player's vision, as he is able to assess situations while confidently knowing exactly the position of the ball.

Young players should be encouraged to practise ball juggling and in the initial stages the ball should be allowed to bounce on the ground and even be played with the hands in between contacts with the feet. This helps build confidence, and at the same time allows the beginner to learn the basics. Ball juggling should be practised as often as possible, building up from simple beginnings to using various parts of the body, but trying to keep the ball from touching the ground. Sequences can be performed by players who have acquired a high degree of juggling skills and who are able to score a high number of contacts before the ball touches the floor. Conditioning to insist that players do not, for instance, use the same part of the body on consecutive touches will make players who are 'one footed' develop touch on other contacts as well. Alternate right and left foot contacts help players to develop a feel for the weaker foot and often an improvement on the weaker side can be developed and maintained. Players who are able to transfer the ball from foot to thigh to head must have developed good balance, otherwise the sequence would not have been possible. Touch can develop into a natural instinct which determines how hard the ball needs to be played to move it from foot to thigh or head. Balance to enable the ball to be kept under control by the constant transference of weight from one foot to

Fig. 9 Individuals, pairs and groups practise ball juggling to improve touch

21

another is assisted by the use of the arms. Young players should always remember their highest personal score in one sequence as a target to be beaten; this way there is always a personal best to be achieved.

Pairs and group practices can also be used where specific techniques can be isolated (Fig. 9). Players respond to challenges and with a little imagination many such sequences can be presented which will prove enjoyable and demanding and this will add to the natural ability they possess. It is always pleasing to witness players, young or old, performing a high standard of ball juggling, particularly when their individual tricks illustrate the knowledge they have acquired on the mechanics of ball control.

First touch

Players must be continually reminded of the importance of the first touch on the ball when trying to gain possession. Too often the ball is either missed completely or not controlled and an opponent wins possession. Unfortunately, many players seem unaware of the problem and the ball is repeatedly presented to the opponents, providing them with an opportunity to score. It is inevitable that the ball will be lost to the opposing team many times during a match, but good sides are those who do not give the ball away through casual play or poor technique, in fact, they rarely lose the ball at all in their own half. Although the first touch of the ball is crucial, many players have never considered the importance of this point at all. (Are you one of these people?) It has never entered their heads because they are usually more concerned with thinking ahead to what they are going to do when they have possession. This is fine, but often they are unable to carry out their decision because their poor first touch puts them into difficulty. If the ball is accepted cleanly and quickly time and space will be gained to give more chance of making a correct selection. A poor touch provides an opponent with a chance of winning the ball, or forcing a hurried decision. A good first touch may provide a forward with time to shoot at goal, or a midfield player a chance to spot the forward in an advantageous position. In the same circumstances a poor touch will allow the defender to win the ball or the midfield player to be 'closed down' making the pass impossible.

It is possible for a coach to improve the performance of players he has never seen play, merely by talking to them! One of the ways would be to make them aware of the importance of the first touch, so that on taking the field they concentrate on this major point. Too many people like to see young players learning only to stop the ball, but this is nonsense. It is very rare that a ball is stopped when making the first touch, so players should concentrate on developing good touch to adjust the ball into a comfortable position away from the opponents.

Some players, although technically able to control an oncoming football, fail consistently to do so in match conditions. Too often, this is because insufficient attention has been applied to the basics. Many technically competent players are regular culprits in this. Sometimes it appears that they are unaware of their failings, and they do not realise how their own personal performance would improve, as well as that of their team, if only a little more care were taken. If you are a player, concentrate on that first touch and if you are responsible for organising a team, remind your players regularly of this vital issue.

An all round game

Perhaps we should examine just why so much importance should be placed on this point. Football is a 360 degree game. By this I mean that it is possible for players to receive the ball from any direction and they then have the choice of moving in any direction they wish to retain possession. At the same time opposing players may approach from the front, side or rear to challenge for the ball and, therefore, players are required to make a continual assessment of the conditions that surround them, whether they have the ball or not. Players should attempt to develop this awareness not only when they are in possession, but also when 'off the ball'. This will assist in finding space and also be a tremendous advantage when receiving a pass.

It will always be an advantage to possess the ability to control the ball quickly because it provides more time to decide the next move. Opponents have less time to move into a challenging position and a speedy control places them at a disadvantage. On the other hand a poor first touch gives the challenging player the opportunity to 'close down' or even dispossess his opponent. It is obvious, therefore, that with time and space at a premium on a football field, players should work to achieve a good first touch. This can only be achieved by practice, practice and more practice. In the early stages players should be taught practices that help to form good habits. This will enable the basic principles of control to be absorbed.

Principles of control

The technique of control is relatively simple to explain, but far more difficult to master. There are only a few basic points to understand and these are appropriate to every controlling contact of the ball, irrespective of the part of the body used. Once these fundamentals have been grasped it only remains to practise.

Move behind the line of the ball

The first step is to adopt a position that provides the platform for success. This means that whenever possible you should move into a position where the ball will at least make contact with you. Too often players have time to adjust to this basic position but, for example, they allow the ball to pass over an outstretched foot. Moving behind the line of the ball provides greater insurance, for the ball will at worst make contact with the body. Moving into line allows a greater chance of controlling the ball efficiently, particularly if a misjudgement is made, or the conditions cause the ball to act in an unexpected manner.

Decide early which part of the body to use

Once behind the ball the speed and flight can be assessed so that a decision can be made on the part of the body that will be employed to control the ball. In practices the technique can be predetermined and the trajectory of the delivery adjusted accordingly. In the early stages the player need not be presented with having to make a decision, for each service will be similar and only when an appropriate understanding of the techniques has been grasped will the receiver be asked to cope with the decisions that a variety of passes will require. The earlier a decision is made the better. The sooner the receiver has assessed the flight the more time he has to adopt a comfortable position to stop the ball with the selected surface. Many mistakes are made when players change their minds on the controlling surface, thereby giving little time to move into the new position.

Relax and withdraw on impact

Having moved into position and decided how the oncoming ball will be controlled the selected surface should be offered to the ball and when contact is imminent the surface should be relaxed and withdrawn. This will take the pace off the ball. Undoubtedly this is the most difficult part and the main ingredient of success is to become proficient in assessing the speed of the approaching ball, to allow the required touch on the ball to be utilised. The only way to gain this understanding is through practice. There are no short cuts and only if you assess the quality of your control by isolating the faults as they occur will you be able to work on the weakness. In the initial stages players should practise controlling the ball without the threat from a challenging player to make sure that they have a sound knowledge of the basic principles.

The first contact of the ball is an extension of the development of touch. Make sure that the controlling surface is relaxed so that the speed is taken from the ball by this cushioning effect. If the surface is hard and inflexible like a wall, the ball will bounce away. So, soften the surface to absorb the pace of the ball – this can only be achieved by withdrawing the controlling surface on impact.

Many young players find difficulty in understanding how this softening of a hard surface can be achieved. Some cannot comprehend how, for instance, the forehead can be used to control the ball. Although it is not a skill that is often used there are occasions when a player in space can bring a head-high ball under control by following the fundamentals.

Please remember that it does not matter if the ball is controlled by the foot, thigh, chest or head, the same principles apply. Try not to cultivate bad habits by being lazy or casual and do not feel that it is easy because your favourite star player makes it seem simple. He is only able to give that impression because he has worked and worked on his ball control. Even he would admit to occasions when lack of concentration or failure to adhere to the basic rules has caused him to appear mediocre.

On most occasions we have time to adjust our position to control the ball in a standard way, but once these few essentials have been fully understood it should be possible for you to make a good attempt at controlling an oncoming football with any part of the body. There will be many occasions when it is impossible to move into the perfect position to control the ball. It may be because of lack of time or because of the proximity of an opponent. In these circumstances we must make the most of our knowledge so that we can make the best of the situation.

In Fig. 10, having moved behind the line of the ball, the player has decided to control the ball with his chest. We can see clearly how he has presented his chest to the ball and then made sure that the ball has been controlled by withdrawing his chest from the ball. His arms have played an important part in making sure he is balanced and you can see how his attitude changes by the forward movement of his shoulders as impact is made.

The same fundamental of withdrawing the controlling surface can also be seen in Fig. 11 as on this occasion the thigh is presented to the ball before being withdrawn to achieve control.

A mark of a good player is one who is able to accept efficiently passes from all heights, speeds and angles. You will find it possible to improve greatly your controlling ability if you follow these very simple rules. Remember, a little thought can make you a better player.

Fig. 10A Move behind the line of flight of the ball

Fig. 10B Relax and withdraw controlling surface on impact

Fig. 11A Player has moved behind ball, offers his thigh

Fig. 11B Thigh is withdrawn on impact

Watching the professionals

In any sport it is always advantageous for those with little experience to watch performers at the highest level. As far as young players are concerned this is an important feature in the learning process, for it often provides the inspiration that is needed for the player to achieve a higher standard of performance.

Having grown up in London, I was fortunate enough to have a choice of first class matches every Saturday. Often I played for my school in the morning before rushing off to the Football League game of my choice in the afternoon. As I did not support any one particular club my decision was usually decided by who was playing for the teams visiting London. It may have been that Len Shackleton, Stanley Matthews, or Jackie Milburn were playing against Chelsea at Stamford Bridge, or that Manchester United's 'Busby Babes' were visiting Arsenal at Highbury. Young players have an opportunity to see star players on television, but even so, every opportunity should be taken to watch the players live.

I remember Fulham having a spell of attractive First Division matches, which encouraged me to be a regular supporter on the terraces of Craven Cottage. During these matches I was able to appreciate the overall ability of many famous players, but often there was one particular facet of the game in which they excelled. Some were excellent headers of the ball, others were able to dribble past opponents with apparent ease, but I became fascinated by the passing ability of the players, and one in particular – Johnny Haynes, the Fulham and England captain.

He was able to find good positions to receive the ball and, because of his ability to control the ball quickly, he appeared to have plenty of time to select his pass. His passing was equally efficient over short or long distances and the ball usually arrived accurately at the correct pace, to provide his team mate with every opportunity to control the ball quickly. You can imagine how privileged I felt when a few years later I found myself in the same Fulham team.

I recall an occasion when shortly after joining Fulham I attended a practice session at Craven Cottage. The majority of the players were gathered in the centre circle where one player was undergoing a fitness test following a leg injury. He was kicking footballs from the halfway line towards one of the goals and intimated that he would try to hit the crossbar of the goal. Needless to say, he failed, but following some light hearted banter he challenged Haynes to do better. The other players looked on and were suitably impressed when his one and only attempt bounced on top of the crossbar. Of course the odds were against him and it was unlikely that he could have repeated the feat – which he sensibly refused to try. Even so, he certainly had more chance of achieving it than any of the others because he had mastered the art of passing and his judgement of distance was unique. One of the major causes of lost possession can be attributed to poor passing, so let us examine the factors that you need to understand and to practise, so that we can fully appreciate the qualities that players of Haynes' calibre possess.

Back to passing

In the early stages young players should receive an abundance of practice in the various techniques of striking a football. Presumably you have a reasonable level of performance in these techniques but I feel that we should give some thought to re-establishing the fundamentals in our minds.

Beginners are able to learn in unopposed practices where they have ample time to think about the technique before it is performed. This is commendable because at that stage we are working to build an understanding into good habits. When initially we move on to expose young players to match conditions such beginners are usually totally absorbed in the competition to make contact with the ball, with little thought being given to the techniques involved. As experience is gained players become more capable of assessing the game and are able to decide upon and

25

attempt to perform a particular skill. The decision may be to volley or head the oncoming ball towards goal or to pass the ball to a team mate. The success that is achieved will be directly linked to the results of our early practices.

Before a pass is made the player must assess the type of pass that is required. Obviously, the distance to be covered and the position of opponents will have a bearing on how the ball will be played and the technique of any pass will vary depending on such things as the condition of the ground.

Players cannot expect to attain a reasonable standard in passing until they fully understand how a ball reacts to the many contacts that it receives. Only when we examine Association Football in depth can we fully realise the varied number of kicking and heading techniques that need to be mastered. There are many books covering the basics of techniques to which you should refer if you find that any particular technique of yours needs to be examined in detail. This book is intended for players who have acquired a reasonable level of skill and who should, in the main, have developed a level of success in the technical application of ballwork.

However, there are guide-lines that can be related to every contact on the ball and we must be absolutely certain that they are understood. This will ensure that we know and understand the mechanics of striking the ball which is essential in attaining success.

Hitting on or above the centre line of the ball will keep the ball down whereas just the opposite will occur if contact is made below the middle line (Fig. 12). Striking the ball on the left side of the ball will cause it to swing to the right and vice-versa (Fig. 13). The flight of the ball can be varied both by the amount of follow-through that is applied as well as the position of the body when contact is made. Generally the ball will stay low if the body is over the ball, but when we require the ball to be played in the air, the player should lean back away from the ball.

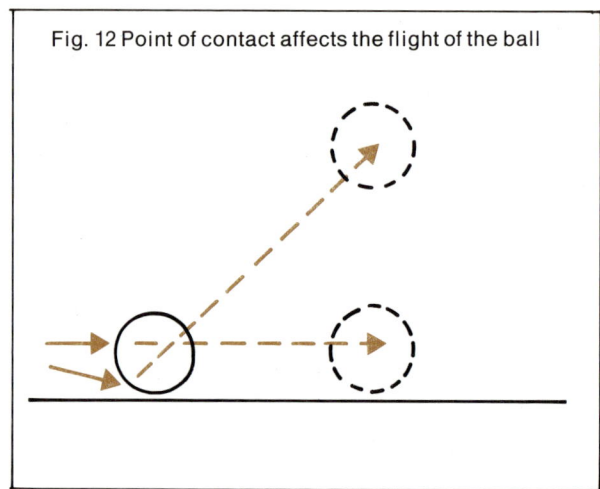

Fig. 12 Point of contact affects the flight of the ball

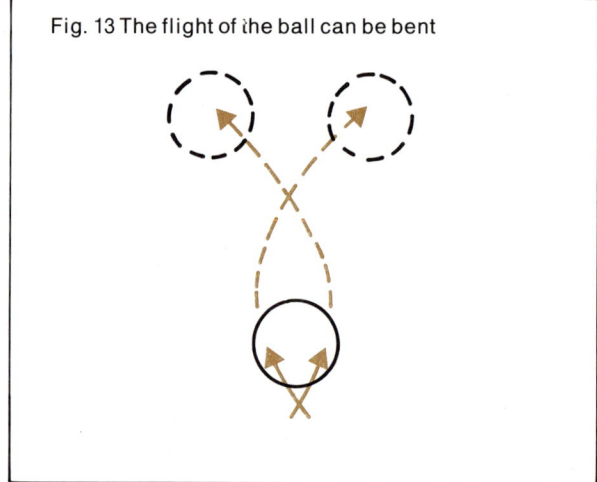

Fig. 13 The flight of the ball can be bent

Accuracy is the fundamental requirement of passing and this is related to the quality of contact on the ball. If the ball is struck in the middle with the striking surface moving along the line between the ball and its target then accuracy is achieved, for the ball will travel in a direct line to its target. There are times when it is desired to move the ball in an arc towards its target and this difficult skill is achieved by striking the ball off centre to impart spin to the ball.

Passes with the inside of the foot have more chance of being accurate than those played with any other surface because the striking area is relatively large as well as being flat. More passes are made in this way than any other and if these passes miss their target it is usually due to one or more of the following reasons:

1   The player has not looked before making the pass
2   The standing foot has not pointed towards the target
3   The foot playing the ball has not followed through in the direction of the pass.

These passes are usually along the ground and have a range of up to 40 metres. Young players in particular should practise this type of pass as it is the most common to the game. There are numerous practices that can be used and I have included some simple examples which can be used by players of all abilities.

Practices
The organisation of practice sessions is governed by the number of players and available footballs. A ball between two is a luxury which is not often possible. Therefore, these simple to organise routines can occupy several players with one or two footballs. Start with one ball being played across a circle of players: the receiver controls the ball before passing to keep the sequence going. When players have achieved a reasonable standard, encourage players to follow the path of the ball. As players improve use two footballs so that players have to look carefully before passing – to make sure that two footballs are not played to one player.

Better players will be capable of passing on the first touch only. If they are unable to play across the circle first time the ball should be controlled and played to their immediate neighbour, who will pass it across the circle on his first touch.

Passing lines are another basic routine which can be adjusted to provide a range of activities. Two groups of players face one another in single file. The ball is played across to the man at the front of the opposite file and then the first man follows the ball and joins the end of the other rank of players (Fig. 14). The distance between the lines can be varied to enable

Fig. 14 Passing lines – easily organised and enjoyable

players to experience the power that is required to move the ball over the required distance.

In all practices it is necessary for players to be aware of making the ball arrive at a speed that is easy to control. In match conditions players have to play the ball firmly enough to bypass opponents without them being able to intercept, but not so hard that the receiver has difficulty in controlling the ball. Whenever possible, passes should arrive at the feet of team mates and all these practices train players in this respect.

The power of *weight* behind the pass can be practised by opening out the passing lines to enable the receiver to be moving towards the ball. If the players are conditioned to at least two touches of the ball, the man opposite the receiving player moves forwards as the receiver makes his first touch. This will have the effect of varying the distance of the pass and players should assess the distance to the oncoming player before *weighting* the pass correctly. In this practice the man is always coming towards the passer and it is not too difficult to play to the feet. It becomes more difficult if the sequence is altered slightly. Players, from one end, instead of moving in a direct line towards the opposite file, now have an option to move left or right at whatever angle and speed they choose. Players now have to *weight* the ball correctly to pass to the feet of a moving player. Vision is important, so players must lift their heads after controlling the ball to assess the direction and speed of the pass.

This type of practice, where there is no opposition, is to help improve technique. The points to work on are:

1   *Controlling* the ball with a good first touch
2   *Deciding* upon the appropriate pass so that the ball can be played *accurately* to *the feet* of the receiver
3   *Weighting* the ball with the appropriate strength to make control as simple as possible for the receiver.

There may be occasions when you need to play the ball in the air. In this case the basic rules should be applied so that you strike below the middle of the ball, with the body leaning away from it.

When the ball is on the ground, kicks with the instep are played with the toe turned downward so that contact is made with the laced part of the boot. Because the area is narrower than the inside of the foot, accuracy is more difficult to achieve. However the advantages are that more power and therefore greater distance can be achieved. Power is produced by the straightening action of the leg and the degree of power is linked to the kicker adopting the correct position.

If the intention is to keep the ball low, the non-kicking foot should be placed near to and to the side of the ball with the head and the knee of the kicking leg over the ball on impact. Sometimes the approach to the ball will be straight-on, but more often a slightly curved approach run is used. This is particularly so when the ball is to be lofted. In this instance the final stride will be long and the standing foot will be placed just to the side and slightly behind the ball. The body should lean slightly sideways and away from the ball to allow the striking leg plenty of room to swing to the ball. A good follow-through will assist in adding power to the ball.

In Figs. 15 and 16 we can see two similar instep kicks being made. The position adopted by the player should tell you his intentions. In the first picture he is leaning over the ball to drive the ball low (Fig. 15). To ensure this happens the ball must be struck in the middle. The second photograph sees the player leaning away from the ball, as he wishes to play the ball into the air (Fig. 16). Contact with the ball should be made beneath the middle line.

Players should practise passes made with the instep to improve the technique for balls played in the air and along the ground. Practices can be conditioned to force players to concentrate on particular points.

As in all passing, the contact on the ball is vital. It never does any harm for players to revert to basic techniques. Whenever players work on techniques it is

Fig. 15 The instep drive: lean forward to keep ball low

Fig. 16 The lofted instep kick: lean back and away from ball

essential that they are motivated to produce a high quality of performance. Too often players fall down on basic factors and this is often because of their poor attitude to the apparently simple aspects of the game.

More practices

1 Players stand 20 to 25 metres apart in twos or threes.
   a) Drive the ball low so that it stays low
   b) Play the football so that it bounces only once before reaching receiver – team leader should indicate how high the ball should be played
   c) Play the ball to be controlled by the chest, knee or foot – concentrate on first touch of receiver as well as technique of kicker. (Players to say where the ball is intended to be controlled *before* the ball is played)

   d) Practise bending the ball from left and right using *both* the inside and outside of both feet
2 With a group of players in an appropriate area, the man in possession plays a long pass to any player who is in space; the receiver controls the ball and plays a short pass to nearest player who controls and plays a long pass to a player in space, and so on. The practice can be controlled to make long passes alternately high and low. Receiving players should be encouraged to attack the ball to make an early control. Lazy players will wait for the ball to arrive so that it has lost momentum. Moving to meet the ball produces a more realistic situation in which players can really test their capabilities and it provides practice in improving the first touch.

Practices of this kind enable coaches to vary the demands. An alternative would be to insist that on controlling the long pass the player plays a short pass to another player, who then can select a long pass, and so on. Players should not be static, but should constantly change their positions so that the picture alters frequently.

The chip

As always there are one or two exceptions to the rule. Normally the body leans away from the ball when it is intended to lift the ball into the air. However, the technique of *chipping* is the exception. When we wish to impart backspin onto the ball in an effort to make it rise steeply into the air and stop quickly on returning to the ground the body weight should be forward. The ball is struck firmly at the bottom of the ball – with as little follow-through as possible.

When the ball is moving towards you the skill is relatively easy as this assists in producing the back-spin. When the ball is moving away from you the skill becomes more difficult and although it may be possible to chip the ball the success rate will be much lower.

When chipping remember to:
1   Move standing foot next to the ball
2   Position head forward over the ball
3   Strike the ball at the lowest point
4   Do not follow through.

The volley

A ball that is struck with a foot while it is off the ground is called a volley and it is one of football's most difficult skills. The easiest of volleys is the defensive volley, where the defender is more concerned with making a clearance than looking for accuracy. In these circumstances contact should be made to the lower part of the ball with the appropriate power to clear the danger. This will send the ball into the air providing time for the defence to readjust.

The most difficult is the volley where the intention is to keep the ball low. If the intention is to perform a low volley in the direction you are facing, it is impossible to strike the ball above the centre line in an effort to keep the ball low. In these circumstances the ball should be allowed to fall as low as time will allow and then you should strike with the instep of the boot and with the toe extended downwards so that contact will be below the middle line, but it is possible to keep the ball low if the follow-through is restricted. When shooting the ball's flight can be bent by striking it with the inside or outside of the foot to impart spin, as previously explained.

When an approaching ball needs to be volleyed at right angles the technique is quite different for it is now possible to strike the ball on or above the centre, to keep it down. If the intention is to volley the ball to your left move into the line of flight, turning your left foot and shoulder slightly towards the oncoming ball. Kick with your right foot across the line of flight, with a full swing of the leg, making contact on or above the middle of the ball with the instep. The swivelling action of the body will assist in providing power to the ball. Volleys can apply tremendous power to the ball with many of the most spectacular goals coming from this exciting skill.

I hope that this brief analysis of the most common skills will re-establish in your mind the importance of understanding the basics.

Support

When training takes place the emphasis is usually concentrated on technique and skill practices with the ball, to equip players for the demands of the full game. For the individual player, however, time with the ball is limited.

As 22 players compete for possession of the ball during 90 minutes of play, it is obvious that no player can expect to be in control of the ball for more than a total of a few minutes during a match. This emphasises why players should work for their highest level of performance with the ball, so they can exploit their small share of possession to the full.

If this is the case, what are players doing for the rest of the 90 minutes? When the opposing team has the ball, players of the defending side are taken up with working to regain possession of the ball. Players of the attacking team are involved in combining to maintain possession, while at the same time looking for the opportunity to attack the opponents' goal. It is this skill that makes the difference between good and poor teams. Teams consisting of players who are good on the ball may not necessarily be successful, for football is a team game and no player can take on an opposing team on his own. We have already discussed football's earliest days, when it was quickly realised that players 'off the ball' should make themselves available to receive a pass as often as possible. It is the sides consisting of skilful players who are able consistently to provide a variety of options for the man 'on the ball' who are the leading attacking teams. All sides need to be adept in defending as well as attacking, but this aspect of the game will be discussed later.

Laymen usually assess players on their ability with the ball, but this is insufficient, for footballers must be good players off the ball as well. With the game being so fluid and with the point of attack continually changing, it requires players to be constantly assessing how they can contribute to maintaining possession. One of the essentials is to support the man with the ball.

The team in possession of the ball ideally requires at least two supporting players to provide an option for the man on the ball. In fact, the whole basis of possession (attacking play) is founded on the series of triangles formed by the deployment of the 11 players. There are times when an individual is in no position to support the immediate play, so he should try to anticipate how the move will develop, so that he is able to offer his support when appropriate. Support can be provided by players a long distance from the ball just as well as those in close proximity. The more players who can find positions to receive the ball at any one time the better the chance of maintaining possession. The man on the ball can then select the pass he feels most advantageous and the fact that he has alternatives makes it more difficult for the opposing team to predict where the ball will be played.

The triangles formed by the players are continually changing and good supporting players offer themselves at the appropriate angle and distance to suit the situation. Players who support from too great a distance or at an angle which makes it impossible for the passer to move the ball accurately, may just as well leave their team mate isolated, because their contribution is negligible. Equally, players who support too closely can often inadvertently assist in losing possession because, should the ball be played to them in a confined situation, they can be pressurised by the opposition (Fig. 17). This often results in a hurried pass being played, and possession is lost.

Consideration must be given to the whereabouts of opponents when assessing where to support. Opposed practices present situations closely related to those which occur in matches and offer players the opportunity of experiencing the problems which exist during a game. There are, however, occasions when despite the lack of opposing players we do not support properly. Before we introduce challenging players we should be certain that players are aware of the ideal positions to support the man on the ball.

I have found the following practice useful. Six to ten players number off and form a circle. If eight players are used No. 1 has the ball and the ball is passed around the circle in numerical order from No. 1 to No. 8, who then plays the ball to No. 1 for the sequence to start again. Therefore, each player *always* passes the ball to the same player and *always* receives the ball from the same player (e.g. No. 3 *always* plays the ball to No. 4 and *always* receives the ball from No. 2). As soon as the players understand the conditions they should be encouraged to be on the move continually, changing their positions within the given area. Once the original circle has broken up players

Fig. 17A Supporting too close, inviting early challenge from opponent

Fig. 17B Selecting correct position provides space and therefore time

must now be aware of the position of the person from whom they will receive the ball. This will help to ensure that a good supporting position is found to allow the pass to be made accurately and quickly.

Players should work to find a position *in front* of the man from whom they will receive and not behind as so often happens. An *early call* to the preceding player *before* the ball reaches him will assist him in adjusting his body position to allow the pass to be played accurately to his feet. The same practice can be used to work on control and basic passing techniques.

The practice will soon show an improvement in the awareness that players have to enable them to find a good supporting position – at the appropriate distance from the passer. Conditioning the routine to encourage players to play one touch when possible, will test the players' ability further in control, pass and support. It can also be adapted to a training routine as well as a technique practice by insisting that the players fulfil exercises after they play the ball. They may be asked to sprint 10 metres or to lie down to place their shoulder blades on the floor before rising and sprinting. Many stipulations simulating the type of inertia which occurs during a full game can be included to test the techniques involved whilst under physical stress. If goalkeepers are involved with the group they should use their hands to field and pass the ball and the player preceding them can be given licence to vary the service to him to simulate the real thing.

Chapter 4 Passing in match conditions

Having examined how important the techniques of control, pass and support are to maintaining possession of the ball, we should now bring them together and relate the topic of passing to the match situation. So far we have explored them as individual aspects and looked at basic ideas to improve the understanding and practical ability at technique level. However, players of all ages and abilities must be exposed to completely realistic situations. Unless players grow up with the problems presented by opponents, they will become tremendous ball players, but disastrous footballers. Opposed practices, to encourage skill, and unopposed practices are equally necessary for players at all levels, but there is no point in presenting inexperienced players with a physical challenge from an opponent until he can perform the technique efficiently.

Gaining confidence

One of the prime objectives in developing talent is to impart confidence to the player. Practices should be set up to allow players plenty of time (space) to undertake the required skill. Players who are confronted by an over competitive situation will never improve and before any practice is set up a great deal of consideration should be given to the number of players being used in relation to the area selected. Small-sided opposed practices using only a few players can quickly expose the problems confronted in matches.

If we use an area of approximately 10 metres square and set three players to retain possession against a challenger the fundamentals are quickly realised. Players off the ball must work hard to provide a good angle for the pass to be made. Even in basic forms of passing, supporting players will hide behind the challenger, making safe passing difficult. They must be educated to show for the ball in the best possible position to receive it (Fig. 18). Often a movement of a metre or two can make the difference between a possible pass and a probable pass. The margin of error should be made as wide as possible to

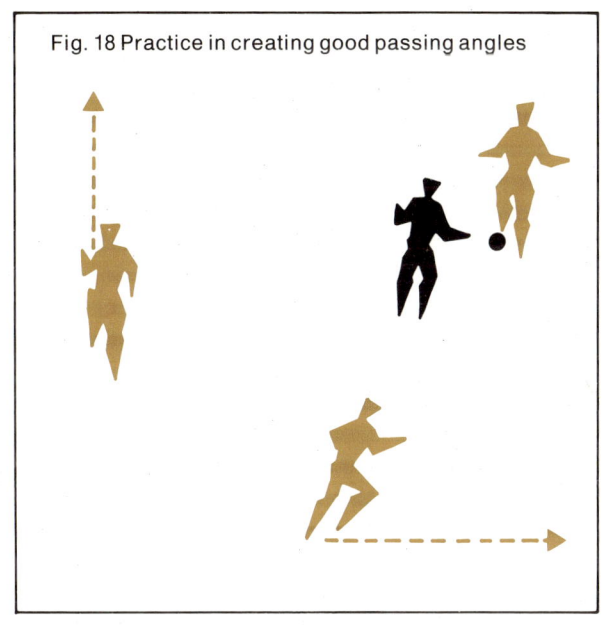

Fig. 18 Practice in creating good passing angles

allow for an inaccurate pass or for the defender to read the direction of the ball. This exercise requires players to work hard at supporting one another. A constant change of position always working to find the best angle and at the same time keeping as far away from the passer as possible will give the best chance of stringing passes together. If the distance between the two players is too restricted the receiver will be closed down very quickly and the sequence will be jeopardised. Supporting at a slightly greater distance will enable the receiver to have enough space to control the ball before selecting the next pass. Control is an important factor and as the area is fairly tight, the first touch of the ball must be relaxed to allow the ball to be retained close enough to guarantee possession.

This routine will also provide an insight and a learning platform in the *timing* of a pass. Opposing players should be committed to the player in possession before the pass is played. If the ball is played too early, or too softly, the challenging player will have a chance to adjust his position to make things difficult

Kenny Dalglish, under pressure from 'Joe' Dwyer, keeps his concentration

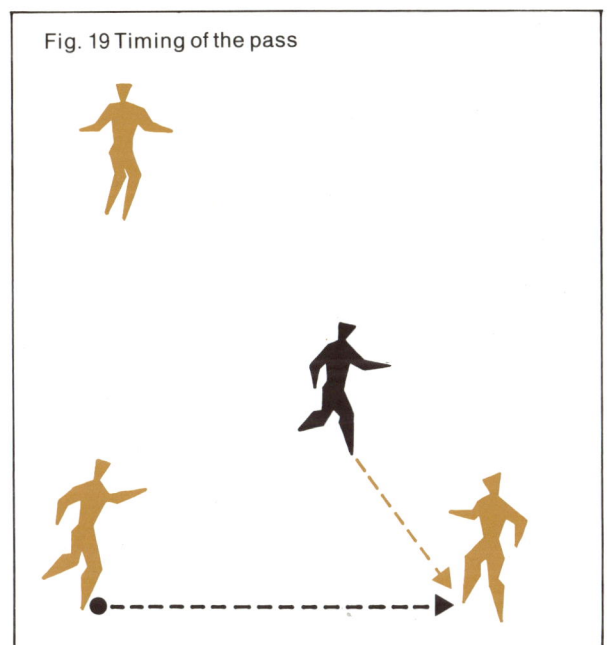

Fig. 19 Timing of the pass

for the receiver (Fig. 19). Equally, if the ball is played too soon the receiving player may not have had a chance to move into position. If the pass is delayed too long the challenger will be able to deny passing possibilities completely. As players gain more experience a feeling for releasing the ball at the correct moment will be developed.

I do not find this practice interesting enough to occupy players for any length of time, but it is an excellent exercise to bring out the basic principles of passing. There are many practices like this, using lopsided numbers and if you are not careful the outnumbered player soon loses interest. Be aware of this fact and think of ways to stimulate the players to produce a high level of play. One method would be to change the roles of the players so that the player who loses possession becomes the challenger. This will motivate the players – the challenger will try harder to win the ball and the three players will try even more not to be responsible for loss of the ball.

Players can be expected to make a great effort in this type of practice. What should be remembered is that it is necessary for players to realise that there is a purpose to the practice and that it should be related to situations that arise during the 11-a-side game. The difficulty is to make players aware of similar circumstances so that they work equally hard in matches as they do in this simple exercise.

During the practice the challenging player should await his chance to win the ball. It may arrive because of poor control or because the pass is not played firmly enough. In addition he will be trying to read or anticipate the thoughts of the men in possession. It is necessary for the passes to be unpredictable so as to make the challenger's task even more difficult. Setting the three players a number of uninterrupted passes as a target will make for a very competitive attitude in the game and will encourage passers to disguise their intentions.

35

Disguise

Disguise is the icing on the cake where passing is concerned, and it is those players who can foster this aspect within their repertoire of skills who become the most skilful. As more players are added, the playing area must be adjusted to allow players an appropriate space. Confined space is not a platform for improvement, except with the very best players. Larger areas providing more space should be used for lesser players.

Although a three against one practice provides the fundamental problems, they become more complex as the combination of players is increased. Three men against two certainly reduces the passing options and requires a considerably higher level of performance. With this combination of players it is unlikely that inexperienced or low quality players will be capable of making many uninterrupted passes, unless the area is increased drastically to enable players to create sufficient space.

Coaches should ensure that their players are subjected to an amount of challenge that will test their ability, but at the same time allow them to achieve a sequence of passes if they perform to their capabilities. Even the best players work in overloaded practices. These confidence-building exercises allow players to practise the touch passes that are vital to good team play. The Brazilians are well known to use practices similar to the following uncomplicated game.

Players form a circle with one challenger in the centre attempting to win the ball as it is passed around and across the circle. Play may be conditioned to one touch, which will place a demand on the performances of the individuals. Passes will have to be accurate and at a pace that will give the receiver a chance to continue the sequence. The touch on the ball will be tested and with an active challenger the circle of players can be encouraged to disguise their passes. When the ball is intercepted the challenger changes places with the player whose pass broke the sequence.

I have found a similar practice with two players in the middle of the circle is an enjoyable test for the players. Players forming the circle must try to maintain possession of the ball. Passing can be tested further by conditioning players to attempt to play the ball between the two challenging players when an opportunity arises. The two challengers score every time they intercept and the passers score when they divide the challengers with a through pass (Fig. 20).

Opposed practices

Training games to improve passing can be programmed to present the required challenge to the players' ability. An opposed practice using, say, seven players against two will be further conditioned by the size of the playing area that is chosen. Seven men against two in a penalty area will mainly invite short passes with an occasional long pass, but if the area is doubled in size a completely different type of pass will be seen. (More passes will be played in the air over longer distances.) When working with such numbers it should be easy for the seven players, but if this is so, a high demand in the number of passes should be set as a challenge to ensure that concentration is maintained. Furthermore, players should try to select the best possible pass. In order to gain maximum effort from the two challengers it is sometimes advisable to change the challenging players every two minutes. This will encourage them to work hard knowing that they will not be exposed to a prolonged effort, which would normally cause them to coast through the session. Competition can be introduced to see which pair of defenders can intercept the greatest number of times during the two minutes. This will provide realism to the practice.

If the players' performance is felt to need a greater challenge then the numbers can be adjusted to make six players play against three or even five against four for good performers.

Players should try to produce a good performance by bearing in mind the various techniques that they have learnt and coaches or team leaders should look for opportunities to help the individuals to improve

Fig. 20 Players enjoying an interesting practice – a point is scored by splitting challengers

their ability. Too often these practices are allowed to degenerate rather than to act as a stimulus for raising standards. Always remember the reason for choosing any particular practice and work on it.

Practices with equal sides have a high transfer value to the game and can be set up to encourage players to maintain possession of the ball. Possession can be made the only issue in a game that is non-directional, where points are scored if a team can make a predetermined number of passes. This number will be related to the ability of the players. The game is simply to maintain possession of the ball within an agreed area. For reasonable players ten passes may be set as the target before a point is won. For lesser players five passes may be considered an appropriate

test. This game produces most of the problems that are confronted in a match and the fact that the sides are even – say eight-a-side – means that control, pass and support can be emphasised to the players. Players with an understanding of these major factors will contribute most to the game.

As the principles of the game hardly alter coaches are always looking for new ways of presenting the game to maintain the interest of their players. The following game is an extension of the previous idea and although the same problems are encountered the players have an option to score in any one of four goals.

The area and number of players will have to be adjusted to suit the available facilities. It may be

37

Peter Nicholas of Crystal Palace – one of Britain's most outstanding young players

possible to gain some benefit from an indoor session if the numbers are appropriate to the area concerned. I have shown the game in an outdoor environment using the area between the penalty area and half way line.

Make four small goals as in Fig. 21 and play six-or eight-a-side. The teams can score in any goal, but they cannot try to score until they have made a pre-set number of passes. This condition not only ensures that both teams work hard in their changing roles of attackers and defenders, but players on the ball nearing the end of the required passes condition

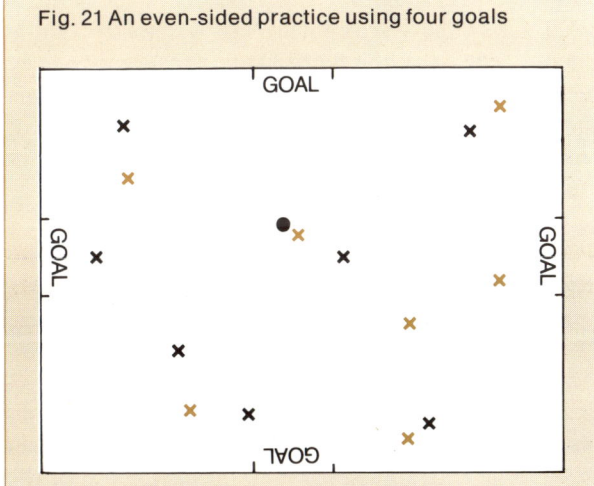

Fig. 21 An even-sided practice using four goals

themselves to seek to transfer the ball to colleagues who have the most chance of scoring in any of the goals. Selection of the pass requires players to be capable of widening their field of vision and this practice poses the problem of assessing which player is in the most advantageous position.

Shortly after signing for Cardiff City I became friendly with a group of young players who played for a 'parks' team. Gradually I became more interested in working with these youngsters because I was impressed by their keenness. During the 10 years that I was associated with Lake United it developed from

a team in the lower divisions of its parks league to election to the Welsh League, the senior league in Wales. During that time I learnt a vast amount and it gave me the opportunity to compare the problems confronted by players at Football League level as well as at a standard more familiar to the average player. One of the fundamental points that was soon appreciated was that nothing could compare with match situations.

The better practice situations provide a high transfer value to the game, to allow skill to be improved. No practice, however realistic, can provide an exact replica of the real game, for there is something special about the excitement that is experienced prior to and during a competitive match. The flow of adrenalin sometimes retards a player's ability, but can also provide the extra stimulation to produce a high quality performance. This is one reason why players who look the part in training can disappoint in their contribution to a match, and others, who are average players during the week's preparation, suddenly emerge as high quality players.

In my experience I have found that the downfall of many technically competent players is linked to the selection of the pass. I wish that young players would examine their own deficiencies in the same way as they criticise others, because this is one way to improve quickly. This was emphasised to me a few years ago with a player from the club I have mentioned. I am sure you could relate this true story to players within your club because it is a familiar case.

Gwynn was an industrious midfield player, totally committed to his club and who was respected by everyone. It soon became evident that his enthusiasm was working against him and that he could have been a much better player than he was. Many times during a game you would hear his team mates say, 'Well played, Gwynn', as he won possession of the ball with a timely, strong tackle. Unfortunately, it was often followed by, 'Bad luck, Gwynn', as a 35 metre pass narrowly failed to split the opposition's defence.

One day I asked a spectator to count the number of occasions that Gwynn actually won the ball himself, during the first half, and also the number of times that he gave the ball away. He won the ball himself 14 times and lost possession on 11 occasions! His colleagues were patting him on the back at half time, complimenting him on his contribution, because it was impossible not to have noticed his enthusiastic performance. The fact that he had lost the ball so many times had not been noticed because they were nearly good passes.

He was surprised to be told of the facts – he just had not given it a thought. The lesson did him the world of good and he has never forgotten it. In the second half he improved his percentage by winning the ball himself on 12 occasions and only losing possession 3 times. This was because he was aware of his problem and in the second half tried to play the ball 'to feet' and reduce the length of his passes. Since that day he became a better player and I feel that he would have been capable of playing in a higher standard – if he had realised the problem a few years earlier.

Selection of pass

Players such as Gwynn must not become negative with their passing. They should be aware of the importance of selecting the right pass and assess when possession must be maintained and when the gamble on a difficult pass is worth the risk. This type of pass, which may be over any distance, is usually played in the attacking third of the pitch where lost possession will allow time for your team to defend properly. Gambling in the defensive third is nothing less than suicide, where safety first should be the theme.

It has already been made clear that successful passing depends on a passer and receiving players, and if the man in possession has no supporting player then he is forced to try to maintain the ball himself or gamble on a hopeful pass. Players become frustrated when they do support, if the man in possession ignores their efforts and loses possession by being dispossessed, or by kicking the ball aimlessly in the hope of achieving the impossible. If players continually ignore the simple pass to supporting players it is not long before they stop making the effort to support.

Players at higher levels are more aware of working to provide basic passing opportunities as continual long passes have greater chance of interception. It is the more experienced player who is prepared to do the simple things at the right time; too often the lower grade player attempts the most difficult skills. Footballers cannot expect their passing to be good over long distances if they are incapable of doing the 'bread and butter' passes of the game. When a player is having a bad day and has difficulty in judging passes, it is sometimes useful to start playing simple passes over shorter distances. This will help in restoring confidence and it will not be long before the appropriate touch on the ball will be restored.

Timing

Patience is a virtue where passing is concerned and teams must be prepared to keep the ball until an opportunity to make an attack arises. Ideally, players should look for opportunities to create a numerical advantage over the opposition. Where such a position is achieved the defending players should be committed by the man on the ball. If the pass is then released at the right time he can be played out of the game. When to hold and when to pass is the question permanently being asked of players and it is this ability that all good passers possess.

Good timing allows defenders little chance to adjust and allows the receiving player to gain possession in the most useful position. Receiving players also contribute to this factor by moving into the best position at the right time. In the example (right), the receiving player must keep on side and form an angle at the right distance to receive the ball so as to make it impossible for the defenders to intercept (Fig. 22).

Players who are showing for the ball must also have a sense of timing. This timing is concerned with

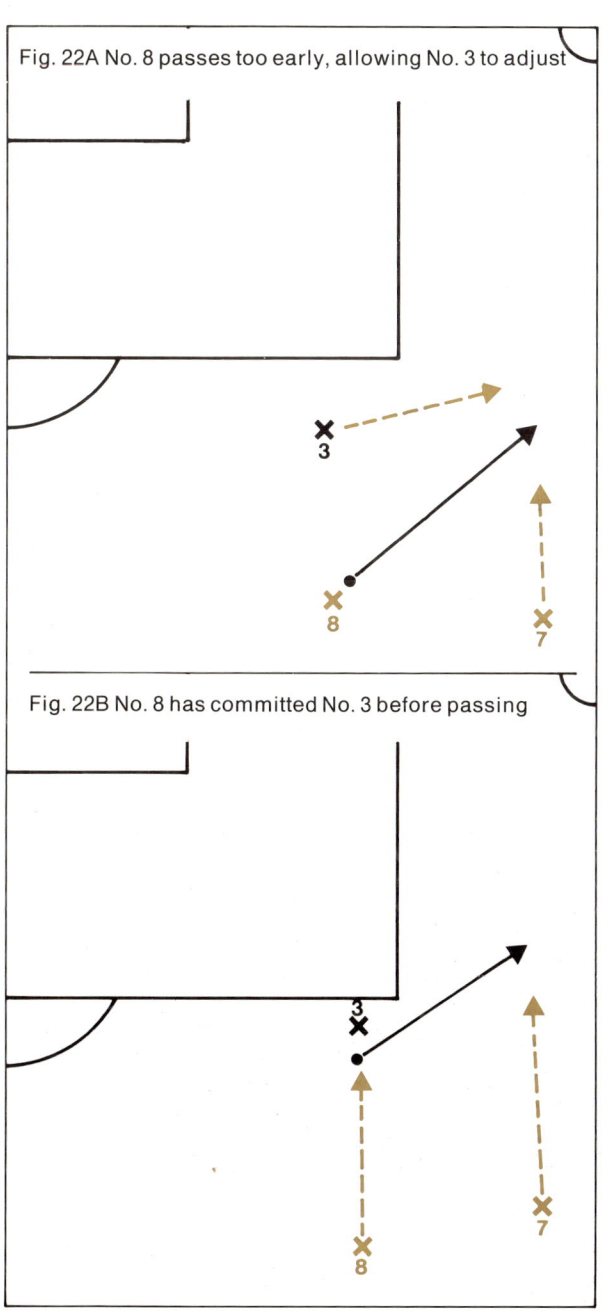

Fig. 22A No. 8 passes too early, allowing No. 3 to adjust

Fig. 22B No. 8 has committed No. 3 before passing

moving into space at the right moment. Moving too early closes the space and not only reduces the target area for the passer, but control has to be exercised in a more restricted area. Receiving players must read when the ball is going to be released so that they move at the appropriate moment.

The time to move can only be gauged if the player on the ball is observed closely. There are moments when, due to the position of the ball in relation to the passer's body, it is quite impossible for the ball to be released. Observing when the picture changes to allow the possibility of a pass provides the signal to move. Moving quickly gives the chance to surprise the defender and time and space is often gained.

I remember playing with one particular player who was not prepared to chase after passes played ahead and always required the ball to be played to his feet. Passes to the feet enable quick control and as he was particularly skilful on the ball it became tactically necessary to bend to his wishes. He was a small nimble winger who was able to drift past opponents, but the first problem was to give him the ball. He had the ability to create space to receive the ball even when he was tightly marked, but it required the passer to possess good timing. When the opportunity arose he would sprint a few metres towards the corner flag, taking the full back with him, as if he required the ball to be played ahead of him. Suddenly he would stop and check back quickly to his original starting point. If the ball was played at the right time he gained possession with enough space to attack the full back. It soon became second nature to me to play the ball to the point from where he started his quick movement and even the most experienced full backs had difficulty in denying him success because if they did ever fail to react they were in a vulnerable position should he have decided to continue his forward run.

Players who played with him for the first time found they reacted by playing the ball to the corner flag as soon as he moved. Even regular team mates were sometimes confused by his convincing act and

41

Terry Yorath and Dai Davies – two truly professional Welsh internationals

occasionally played the ball forward before realising the mistake. When this happened it made everybody involved look foolish, but once an understanding was made it became a very useful ploy.

Square passes

Square passes can provide the most telling attacking opportunities but, equally, can be the most disastrous. The fact that two players are level with each other means that should the pass be intercepted at least two players are out of the game. Sometimes players receive such advice as 'never pass the ball square'. Of course this is nonsense because this type of pass is vital if teams can patiently build up their attacks. Players supporting from behind the ball often move up to provide square passing opportunities and, indeed, often shots at goal can be set up by a square pass.

Players should, however, be aware of the dangers of this pass and extra care should be taken to make sure that there is little risk of interception. Sometimes the receiving player may lose possession of the ball due to poor control and should this occur the situation will be more critical the nearer to the defenders' goal that it happens. Therefore, square passes should be restricted in the defensive third of the field. Players at the highest level have the ability to play such passes, but even so it is possible to see an occasional error which places their goal in jeopardy. Average players should be discouraged from making square passes, unless the risk is minimal.

Square passes played away from the goal, towards the touchline, do not contain as much risk as passes played in the opposite direction. Should the pass break down there is more chance of defenders re-adjusting the covering positions. In addition, more time can be gained to enable defensive players to move goal-side of the ball and even if this is impossible the player will be attacking the goal from an angle.

Two touch football

It is not surprising that teams consisting of players with a high level of ability are able to produce passing movements containing several passes. This is certainly not the case in lower grade football where players are incapable of producing the same quality of possession. An outstanding feature of passing in good teams is the low number of touches that each player has before playing the ball to a team mate. For this to be possible players must have mastered all the components of passing. Players off the ball must support early to offer the receiving player the option of playing a one touch pass. A sequence of passes, quickly changing the point of attack, asks questions of the opponent's defensive qualities which are difficult to answer.

Practice games conditioning players to a maximum of two touches each time they receive the ball force players to support the man with the ball. Unfortunately, players who work hard in conditioned practice sessions do not always show the same commitment in matches. Players should take the field and imagine that the game is conditioned to two touches as this will ensure that they work hard to support their colleagues.

A good player is usually aware of the situation around him before the ball arrives and if a supporting player is available he will possess the ability to move into the best position to lay the ball off first time. Players of lesser ability more often assess the situation *after* they have received the ball and even on the occasions when they are aware of the supporting player they may take too much time in controlling the ball, allowing opponents the opportunity of making the pass impossible.

Many teams use two touch practices within their preparation, but before they commence the players must understand the reason for the condition. *Support* is an obvious requirement and should occur naturally when players realise how restricting life is for the man with the ball. A good first touch is required whether it be to play the ball first time to a team mate or to *control* the ball to enable the pass to be performed easily before the challenge is made by an opponent. If the receiving player has only two touches

43

it is imperative that the ball is delivered so that it is relatively easy to *control*. All these features have been covered, but this type of practice re-emphasises the importance of each.

One of the problems of this practice, especially when regularly included in indoor sessions, is that it mainly encourages a pattern of short passes. In addition, players are forced to pass the ball when normally the situation may be best to hold on to it or to dribble at or past an opponent. Therefore, when players return to the environment of the game it is realised that the transfer value is low as far as team play is concerned. Players need to practise passing so that there is an option of long or short passes to provide them with the opportunity to lift their heads to assess the situation, enabling the right selection to be made.

If, during a match, two or three players keep possession by playing a series of short passes to each other, it often has the effect of drawing opposing players towards the ball. It is then that players away from the ball should look for chances to provide an opportunity for the man on the ball to select a longer pass, changing the point of attack (Fig. 23).

In Fig. 23 three players have played a series of one or two touch passes. The opposing players have been attracted to them. X3 has timed his run to move forward and X4 has changed the play with a long pass into space for X3 to counter-attack. By playing a series of short passes it provides players away from the ball time to adjust into showing position. The onus is now on the player with the ball to have observed situations away from the ball which can be exploited.

Once again I am referring to the selection of the pass, which is just as important as any of the other features of passing.

As you become more experienced you will find that you are able to assess situations to enable you to dictate to the receiving player where the next pass should be made. Good players are able to read the game and visualise moves ahead of the immediate play – just as competent chess players build an attack.

This is often the deciding factor in selecting a particular pass. Players should seek to pass the ball where the opportunity to build an attack exists and this ability to recognise supporting situations is another element in the competent passer's make up.

In Fig. 24, X5 could have played a pass to X11, but instead has assessed the possibilities and has seen that X2 can support X9. Consequently, the pass has been made dictating to the receiver that he should pass to X2, who has moved in support. On some occasions the pass may be played in such a way to emphasise the point. By this I mean that it could be played to the head of X9 where anything other than a headed pass to the supporting player is practically impossible.

Obviously, two-touch practices have a place in preparing players, but please try to understand the reasons for the conditions and be aware of the habits that can be formed by constantly playing in such games. I personally prefer to be selective in asking certain players to play two touch while others play normally. I may allow any player as many touches as he wishes if he stays close to the touchlines with the ball. Often this relates to wingers whom I would wish to encourage to run with the ball at defenders, particularly in the attacking third of the pitch. Players with the ability to take the ball past defenders need to be confident on the ball and I feel that constant two touch football would be detrimental to the acquisition of this confidence.

Allow me to recap on why high level players are able to play a high percentage of one or two touch passing sequences:

1 Because other players support
2 Because they see and have assessed the passing possibilities before the ball arrives
3 Because they possess sufficient skill to play the ball first time – even if it means improvising or adjusting their position quickly
4 Because the ball has been played to them properly – making them favourite to win possession – often dictating the next pass.

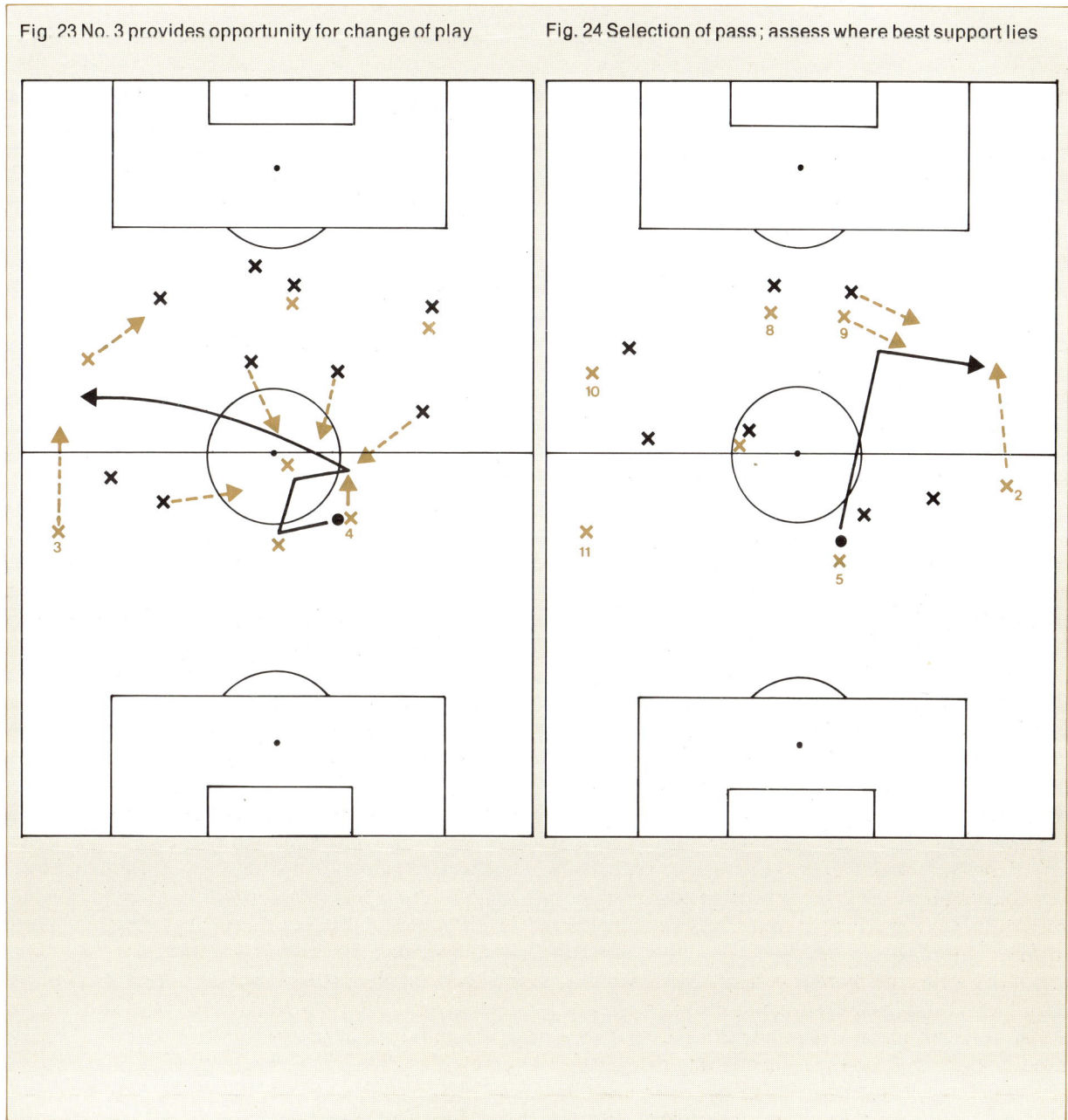

Fig. 23 No. 3 provides opportunity for change of play

Fig. 24 Selection of pass; assess where best support lies

Magic moments by Laurie Cunningham

A typical Kevin Keegan change of direction

Chapter 5 Principles of play: Defence

Principles in any walk of life are the guiding fundamentals on which we build. This is certainly true in Association Football, where the combined functions of individual players must be blended together to produce the foundations of team play. Although the game has changed in many ways over the last 50 years, particularly with regard to systems of play, the principles have remained constant.

Good players act naturally to given situations because they have a particular talent for the game, but I am convinced that if young players examined the primary essentials in more depth, they would develop into better players. Too often players are competent in their own particular position, but are inadequate when faced with an unfamiliar role. We must break down the feeling that players are attackers or defenders because they must have an understanding of both defensive and attacking principles. When our team has possession of the ball we all become attackers and when it is lost an understanding of defensive principles will assist in regaining possession.

Passing, or more specifically *control, pass* and *support,* which has been fully discussed in Chapter 3, is the basis of attacking play, but before we explore the principles of attack let us examine the other aspect of play – *defence.*

Principles of defence

If we accept that the principles are the relationship between players it highlights that players must work as a unit. Once possession has been forfeited, 11 players must be prepared to work together for the common cause of regaining possession of the ball. The most vulnerable time for a defence is when responsibilities change from attack to defence. It is at this point that players are likely to lose concentration and if their minds do not react quickly enough they may present the opposition with an opportunity to score. Mental alertness is as important as physical speed. If you are able to assess situations quickly and react accordingly this will present you with an advantage over your opponent. Therefore, try to avoid the time lag caused perhaps by admiring your shot that almost scored or remonstrating with a colleague over a misdirected pass. Most of all be conscious of this danger period because awareness may enable you to win back possession immediately, or at least deny your opponents a telling counter-attack. With 11 players possessing this quality there is every chance of building a sound defence.

Blanket defence

During recent years, when matches played over two legs have become commonplace, many teams have been more concerned to prevent the opposition from scoring. This has been particularly so when the 'away' side have been the under-dogs and they have based their slim hopes on forming a 'blanket' defence. As soon as sides of this type lose possession they immediately work to manoeuvre all their players back into a deep position, challenging their opponents to break down their defence. Fig. 25 illustrates the area from within which the vast majority of goals are scored.

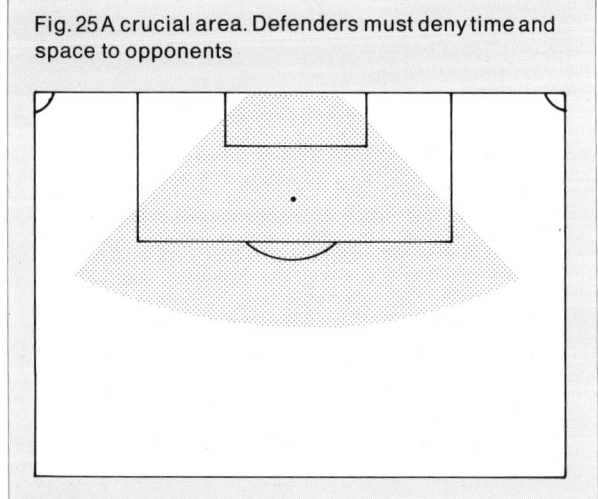

Fig. 25 A crucial area. Defenders must deny time and space to opponents

If the defending team can retreat in numbers to, in and around, the shaded area, this will make any penetrating moves extremely difficult. This form of defence will deny space and time to the attacking team and provide them with little opportunity to produce a strike on goal. Teams prepared to compete in this way make life very frustrating to their opponents. It requires an extra piece of skill to break down such a defensive barrier and often teams are reduced to playing long high passes into the penalty area from which it is difficult to win any quality possession. Furthermore, it may be possible for the defending team to encourage the attackers to press forward, making themselves vulnerable to a quick break.

Even in the most one-sided of matches the outplayed team can usually be relied upon to produce at least one or two chances. This is another attraction of the game because if one of these few opportunities can be converted into a goal and the defence can continually defend in numbers, there is no reason why a surprise result cannot be gained.

The decision to play in this way may be considered very negative, but the basic reasons for the tactic should be understood by all players. Denying space around the penalty area by retreating players is used by all successful teams and this is not necessarily a negative form of play. Even attack-minded teams usually withdraw players to form a defensive block in this way and it requires players to be very fit to enable them not only to return to bolster their defence, but to springboard forward to form and support their attack. This *concentration* of defenders lends its name to the principle that has thwarted even the most successful attacking teams.

Team work

Working to gain as much time as possible for your team to form a strong defence should be uppermost in the minds of defenders. Players should look for opportunities to *delay* attacks in all areas of the pitch. This can only be achieved by stopping opponents from shooting, passing or dribbling the ball towards the goal and it requires players to accept the collective responsibility of closing down attackers. Team work requires players to support each other in many ways.

When dealing with passing I referred to players finding positions to provide the man on the ball with a passing option. This is an essential of attacking play and equally vital is support or *cover* in a defensive sense. When a defender moves to close down his opposite number one of his concerns is that he may be taken on and beaten. If a team mate moves in to cover his challenge the vulnerability of being exposed is considerably reduced.

Good attacking teams which patiently build their raids are able quickly to change the play to produce a new point of attack. Defences must be aware of the danger of being caught lopsided, which would make them vulnerable. For a team to be able to cater for any eventuality it must deploy its players not only to provide strength against the immediate assault, but also to enable a quick adjustment to be made to repel a change of play. A defence which is capable of catering for any required adjustment is said to be *balanced*.

Knowing when and when not to tackle is something which comes through experience. However, this is an area where many good defenders have been caught out. The point that should be remembered is that although a defender may dominate his opponent, it may only be necessary for him to be beaten once in a full 90 minutes for the game to be lost. Defenders should not commit themselves before they need to – unless they are certain of winning the ball. Ideally, *cover* should exist before any risk in challenging is taken. This is particularly so when playing against a skilful opponent when a show of *restraint* will benefit the team.

Some teams try to win the ball back quickly, even in their attacking third of the pitch, by an early challenge supported by other players (Fig. 26).

Here we have a situation where the goalkeeper has gathered the ball in the face of a challenge from X9. He has thrown the ball to his full back (X2) who has moved towards the touchline. The opposing team have worked in unison to close down X2 and other

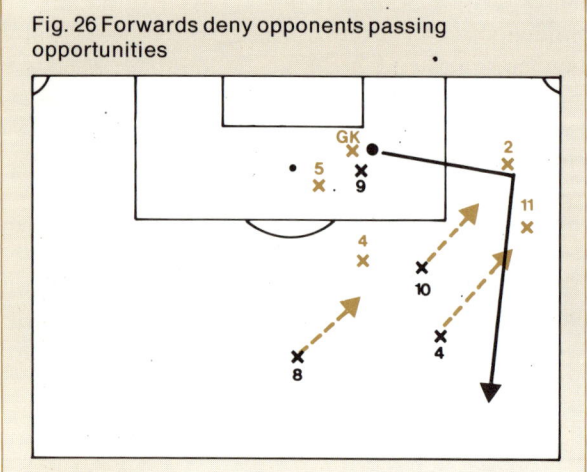

Fig. 26 Forwards deny opponents passing opportunities

Over the last twelve years I have worked on numerous courses for people wishing to become qualified in coaching. During that time it has been my experience that those attending such courses have much more difficulty in totally understanding the principles of play than when dealing with tech-

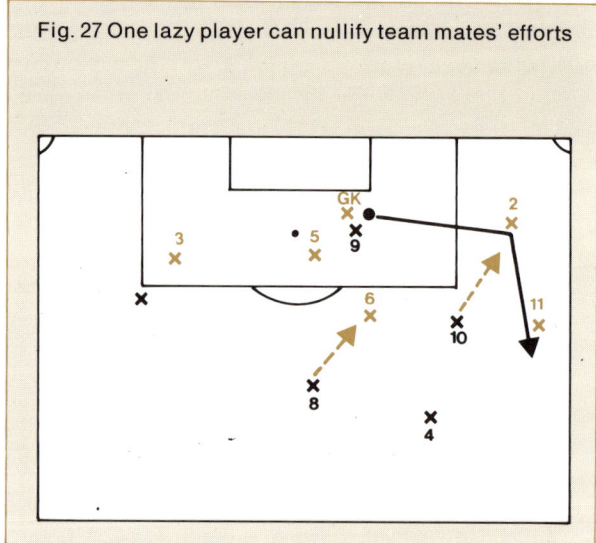

Fig. 27 One lazy player can nullify team mates' efforts

passing possibilities. With the route back to the goalkeeper denied by X9 the full back is forced to play a long hopeful pass which has little chance of reaching its target. This is an example of the defending team working together even in the attacking part of the field of play.

It is vital that players combine to make matters difficult for the opposition because it only needs one player not to fulfil his role for the efforts of others to be wasted. In the same situation if X4 had been lazy or had not understood the situation it would have presented X2 with an easy and effective pass, which could lead to a concerted attack (Fig. 27).

If this situation occurs often players who are prepared to work to pressurise opponents soon realise how ineffective their efforts are and, consequently, their enthusiasm and endeavour is quickly destroyed. Usually teams who are prepared to work for the ball in this way will use similar tactics to win the ball while retreating towards their own goal. By working to win the ball on 'the way back' they try to work to move goal-side of the player, for whom they are responsible, and of the ball, in order to deny passing opportunities to their opponents and to form a strong line of defence.

niques. No doubt this area of the game does require more thought because rather than dealing with an individual it requires an overall understanding of the combined functions of players. I suspect that it is natural for students of the game to find the principles difficult to comprehend, but I have always been concerned that it may have been through my own personal deficiencies in explaining and demonstrating them.

Over recent years I have considered different approaches and have finally settled for a method of presentation which is certainly uncomplicated and which I believe is easy for players to understand. It also allows coaches more easily to identify the roles of defensive players as individuals and in their responsibilities to each other. So let us examine the principles of defence in more depth.

When the ball is lost an instant decision must be made by defenders in the close vicinity to the man in possession – should he be challenged? The nearer to the defenders' goal that the ball is lost, the more essential that the man with the ball should be challenged. Attackers should not be allowed time and space in their attacking third of the pitch and this has been brought home many times during the last few years in some international matches seen on television, where many tremendously spectacular goals have been scored from way outside the penalty area, by players who initially took control of the ball near to the halfway line. On many occasions the players concerned have not had to beat any opponents to reach their shooting position, for the defenders have retreated in front of them to form a *concentration* of players on the edge of the penalty area. This has not been sufficient for it has allowed the attackers to move into range of the goal from where they have punished the defence for not having presented a challenge early enough.

Three types of defender

Players must become aware of the dangers of allowing an opponent to have unopposed possession of the ball and must understand the responsibilities attached to the challenging player. I call a player who makes a challenge on an opponent with the ball the *No. 1 defender*. The challenge can be made in any area of the field of play and by any member of the team.

When the challenging player tries to close down an opponent he should be supported by players who provide *cover*. Covering players are my *No. 2 defenders* and those players, usually behind the ball, who are away from the immediate action but who are responsible for providing *balance* to the defence, are my *No. 3 defenders*.

Breaking their roles down allows us the chance to examine them in depth, but it should be remembered that their reactions are related to each other at all times.

No. 1 defender

Before any player decides to make a challenge on an opponent he should have assessed the situation. There are times when a challenge merely plays into the opponents' hands and it is better to resist the temptation (Fig. 28). Here we see a forward (X9)

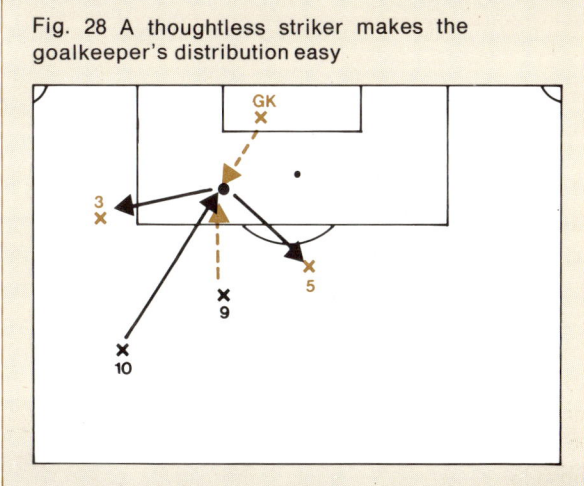

Fig. 28 A thoughtless striker makes the goalkeeper's distribution easy

chasing a through ball which has been safely gathered by the goalkeeper. He does not appreciate the situation and continues forward to challenge, leaving the goalkeeper with at least two simple options safely to distribute the ball (X5 and X3). Had he assessed the situation he would have checked his run or stayed in a position where he could make it impossible for X3 or X5 to receive the ball safely. Then the goalkeeper would probably have been forced to kick a long ball upfield, presenting his opponents with an even chance of winning possession. The decision to challenge the goalkeeper may have been acceptable had other players been available to mark X3 and X5.

A similar situation occurred in Fig. 27 where there would be no point in X10 challenging X2 had X4 not worked to close down X11. Therefore, it can be seen that even before a decision is made to close down an opponent, an awareness of surrounding players is vital.

51

Closing down

Before players are asked to close down opponents they should understand exactly what they are trying to do. It is common to see defending players running from one attacker to another, expending a great deal of energy, but causing the opponents very little concern. The first question to be answered is why close down at all. Every defender realises the importance of this in and around the penalty area when the goal is immediately threatened. Even so, many approach the problem in the wrong way as there are some crucial factors in the manner in which the challenge should be made. Obviously, the closer to the goal that the opponents have the ball, the greater the importance of the quality of the challenge. However, the essential details are similar no matter where the challenge is to be made. The responsibilities of the No. 1 defender start as soon as the decision is made to close down the man in possession and he must understand the basic criteria involved.

The first thoughts are to deny the opponent an immediate attack on goal. If he can be pressurised properly it will provide other defenders the chance to adopt supporting positions to strengthen the defence. In other words we should try to *delay* the man playing the ball forward. With a little thought it becomes possible to make him play the ball in the direction we wish, by reducing the options open to him. This will assist supporting players who will adjust their positions accordingly.

Ideally, we should work to move within two metres and on the goal-side of the man with the ball. The manner in which we approach is vital, because while it requires that we move quickly we must not allow our speed of approach to work against us. If our movement is uncontrolled it will be easy for a good player to side step and move the ball past us. We must be sure not to 'sell' ourselves in this way and we must practise closing down opponents until we have recognised just how quickly and how close we can safely come. The distance between the No. 1 defender and the receiver should, if possible, be made up while the ball is in flight.

One of the governing factors in this matter is whether the man has possession of the ball or if, in fact, he is about to receive it. If he is in possession it is more difficult to be effective and the only chance we have is to hope that other team mates can mark tightly, denying him passing opportunities, or that he becomes careless with his control of the ball. In any event once the decision has been made we should try to move in as close as possible. The nearer we can go, the more difficult it becomes for him.

Young players must learn that unless they move close enough to threaten the man in possession their energy has been wasted. Players often work extremely hard to move within 10 metres and then stop! From that distance there is no danger to the opponent. He can still see past you to observe the passing possibilities being provided by the movement of players and, indeed, select and play any pass that he wishes, and when he wishes! By moving closer it places a threat to the ball forcing his body posture to alter; he will drop his head, thereby reducing his field of vision, as he now has to concentrate on the ball. In addition, passing possibilities will be reduced, for the tighter you make the situation, the less room there is available to play the ball past you.

Interception

One of the main ways of winning possession of the ball is through interception. Alert players often win the ball purely because they are looking for this possibility. When marking an opponent, defenders should try to anticipate when the ball may be passed to him, then as the ball is played, an early assessment will help in deciding if it is possible to intercept the pass. When to attempt to win possession is the dilemma that defenders continually have to answer because an unsuccessful attempt at interception or tackle can provide the opposition with a scoring chance. Players should not commit themselves until their defence has had time to provide *cover*. Often a defender who *delays* his opponent for a few seconds, before being beaten, has made a significant contribution to his defence, because he has made it possible for another defender to move into a supporting position.

It is a common situation for the receiving opponent to gain possession with his back towards the defender. If, as a defender, we can move quickly into a close position to our opponent we may be able to stop him turning. Obviously, this will delay his progress up field and, therefore, we must work hard to prevent him facing us. By pressurising in this way, it may be possible to dispossess him, but in any event he should be forced to play the ball back or across the field, which will in effect cause a delay in the opponent's attack.

If we are unable to move within a few metres of our opponent before he receives possession we are placed at a disadvantage. The greater the distance between the attacker and defender the stronger the position of the forward because he can make unopposed progress. As defenders we should attempt to restrict the opportunities that forwards have to run at us with the ball, because we are then placed at a disadvantage. Closing down attackers limits dribbling possibilities because players are made to stop, thus eliminating their opportunity of running towards the No. 1 defender.

The *angle of approach* should be considered in an attempt to reduce the alternatives open to the forward. By moving in a direct line between the attacker and the goal the opponent is presented with the option of moving the ball past us to the left or to the right (Fig. 29A). If we move across slightly to one side we open up an invitation to the attacker on one side, but at the same time we 'close the door' on the other (Figs. 29B and 29C). In this way defenders try to dictate to the forward where he must move. This not only enables defenders to move opponents into tight situations, but also assists covering players to support the challenge so that the forward has little chance of beating them.

The angle of approach is usually dictated by the covering player, who should communicate to the No. 1 defender indicating whether the opponent should be forced to move outside or across the field of play. Even if a supporting player has not had time to move into position, No. 1 defenders should still try to dictate to the forward in an attempt to push him away from goal into an area where his options are restricted. A deciding factor may be related to the knowledge that we have of our opponent.

Fig. 29A Wrong: defender offers two options to his opponent

Spotting the weaknesses

One ploy is to force attackers to move the ball onto their weaker foot. For instance, if a right winger is particularly good at crossing the ball then it may be a sound tactic to try to make him move inside in an attempt to push him farther across the front of the defence, keeping him with the ball on his left foot. On the other hand, a right-sided player who is fond of

53

Fig. 29B Right: defender invites his opponent to move inside

Fig. 29C Right: defender forces his opponent to move outside

moving inside his full back to shoot at goal with his left foot, may be encouraged to move down the line.

Young players should use their powers of observation to assess the abilities of their opponents. When watching young players it is obvious that many do not understand how vital this can be. It may be that a defender is continually deceived by the same piece of skill, but still he reacts as if seeing it for the first time. His opponent may only be able to go on the outside, but he does nothing to force him onto his weaker side. Therefore, try to assess the strengths and weaknesses of players in the other team and with a little collective thought from team mates even the most dangerous of opponents can be restricted in their contribution.

Other points that should be practised are related to the attitude of the body when challenging. Try not to adopt a square-fronted approach because this makes turning quickly very difficult. When forcing an opponent to move in a particular direction take on a half-turned position in the direction that you are pushing your opponent. This will provide you with a metre's start should he try to burst past you. The next time you see a top-class full back jockeying his winger, take note of his body position and you will see that he is slightly crouched, with legs bent, to enable him to move quickly when required to respond to the challenge. If you do try to force a player in a particular direction you *must not* allow him to check back to beat you on the other side. This is likely to cause your defence a problem as the covering player will be in a position where he is unable to adjust quickly enough to present a challenge. Attackers will be looking for this opportunity, but if you are aware of this possibility the advantage should be with you.

Young players should be aware of the importance of keeping their feet. Too often players fall over unnecessarily when they challenge for the ball and it is easy to form such a bad habit. Of course there are occasions when there is no alternative and at times players should be applauded for their skill in performing such tackles efficiently. This type of tackle has been perfected by many players who use it not only to dispossess opponents by knocking the ball away, but also for taking possession of the ball themselves.

Sliding tackles seem to be a favourite of youngsters, but they should be used only as a last resort or when you are very confident of winning the tackle. Understand that when you are on the ground you are temporarily out of the game. The few seconds needed to regain your feet can be very costly indeed! Fatigue plays an important part in the outcome of matches and a great deal of energy is used up throughout a match by those players who are continually falling over and who must work quickly to get up and recover their positions.

Practices

No. 1 defenders need to work on adjusting their position quickly, particularly when faced by an attacker dribbling the ball. They are often required to do so while retreating in front of an opponent. I find the following exercise useful in providing players with practice in jockeying an opponent:

The players should pair off and one player dribbles the ball forward slowly. The ball should be moved from side to side in a meandering motion while trying to 'sell dummies' to the defending player. The defender retreats slowly approximately two metres in front of his partner while continually adjusting his position to keep in front of the ball. He is prevented from attempting to win the ball until the attacking player decides to try to pass him. Working in a channel five to eight metres wide with the attacker mainly concerned with 'working' his partner this can be a demanding exercise.

The following practice provides defenders with opportunities to work on delay and the angle of approach. A channel is marked out as a boundary and two attackers play against one defender, plus a goalkeeper. The width of the area depends on the age and experience of the players and should be wide enough to test the defender, but not so wide that the attackers' task is too easily accomplished. The defender works hard adjusting his position while the attackers try to score. It is surprising how difficult a good defender can make it for the attackers, who should not move into an offside position.

The practice is particularly valuable when the channel approaches the goal from an angle, rather than straight on. The defender jockeys, trying to dictate to the attackers when the ball should be played. This will help him anticipate when the ball will be passed in order that a quick adjustment can be made. His priority is to avoid being beaten on the inside, which will open up the shooting angle. By being aware of his angle of approach it is not long before the attackers are forced to work extremely hard to score. It may be that the defending player will be unsuccessful in stopping the creation of a shot. He will, however, have achieved a degree of success if, by understanding his role, he has been able to delay the forwards' attack. In match conditions this would have allowed a recovery run to be made by a supporting defender. The routine will provide every chance for the defender to experience the problems confronting a No. 1 defender.

No. 2 defenders

One of the arts required of the footballer is to provide the correct response to the movement and reactions of team mates and opponents. Good players with the ability to read the game are more likely to be in the right place at the right time because they are capable of assessing situations early and they react accordingly. One of the most critical aspects is for defending players to assess when a colleague needs support or cover.

55

It has been established that many goals are scored because players have not supported the challenge of the No. 1 defender. Sometimes the No. 1 defender has been unable to delay the attacker long enough to allow covering players time to move into a supporting position. On other occasions players have had ample time to support but have either failed to recognise the danger of the situation or their support has been in-effective. Everybody recognises the need to challenge the man on the ball. Unfortunately, this same im-portance is not attached to supporting the initial challenge. Often it is only after the challenging player has been beaten that the danger is realised and then, of course, it is too late!

Players who support the challenging player are my No. 2 defenders, so let us look at some of the relevant points that should help you to understand how your contribution to the team's overall perform-ance can be improved. Once again awareness is required of all defending players to adjust to the ever changing pattern of play. As soon as a team mate moves in to present a challenge to the man in possess-ion he should be supported. If it is felt that there are insufficient defenders to mark all opponents it would be unwise to commit yourself to a marking role and under these circumstances a half-mark and half-supporting position should be adopted.

If two of the defending team are confronted by three opponents in their opponents' half of the pitch it may be considered unwise for either one to commit himself as a No. 1 defender. If this happened his colleague would have the problem of moving into a position where he could cover the challenge and be ready to close down either of the other two opponents.

The angle of approach made by the challenger should have been considered for it may have been possible to block one of the passing alternatives, allowing the supporting player to move closer to the remaining opponent, giving more chance of winning the ball or closing down efficiently.

The game is constantly changing along with the roles of the players. If a supporting player (a No. 2 defender) moves in to challenge an opponent who has been given the ball, his responsibilities transfer from a No. 2 defender to those of the No. 1 defender and this small point illustrates how quickly the mind of a player must function.

One of the most disappointing features to occur is when two defenders are beaten by one attacker. The responsibility must rest on the supporting player's shoulders and players cannot be expected to react efficiently to the dual problems of mark or cover unless they understand the problems of covering a challeng-ing player.

Communication between players is a necessity and I am always saddened when young players are rebuked for trying to help each other in this way. Later on I will discuss communication in more depth, but now let us see how it can aid in providing cover.

We have already seen that challenging players should delay attackers until support arrives. There-fore, it makes sense that supporting players should make the No. 1 (challenging) defender aware of their presence. This will provide confidence to the No. 1 defender who can now feel secure and if the chance arises he can attempt to dispossess the opponent. If you are the No. 2 defender you can further help the challenger by encouraging him to make the attacker move in a particular direction. This will enable him to adjust his angle of approach and make it possible for your position to be defined.

In Fig. 30 we can clearly see how the position of the No. 1 defender can present a different problem not only to the attacker (X11) but also to the No. 2 defender (X2). In 'A' the challenger has presented the attacker with the chance of going left or right due to his straight approach. X2 the No. 2 defender has moved slightly to the goal-side, as this is where the main danger could occur. In fact the position of X2 is the factor most likely to influence the attacker's decision on which side to take on X4.

In 'B' this situation is completely different. The No. 2 defender (X2) has encouraged his No. 1 defender (X4) to force the forward on the outside. This has allowed X2 to move across to supply a second line of defence should X4 be beaten.

In 'C' the defenders are trying to make the attacker move inside, perhaps onto his weaker foot where X2 is positioned to back up X4's challenge.

ities. Although it is still related to angles and distances it now must be applied not only to the opponent with the ball but also to other opponents as well. In a straightforward two against two contest, one defender challenges the man with the ball while the other assumes a position where he can cover the challenger, but at the same time offer an immediate challenge should the ball be played to the other forward. Earlier

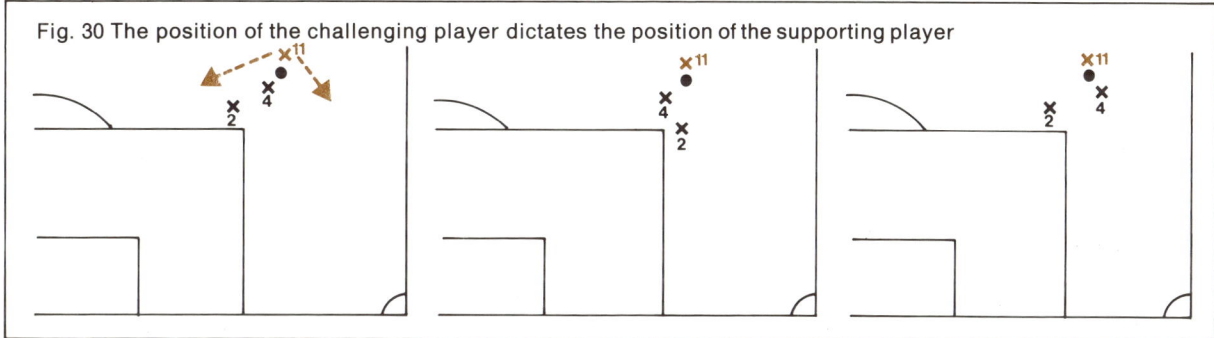

Fig. 30 The position of the challenging player dictates the position of the supporting player

The angle of support should be considered along with the distance that the defender should be behind the challenging player. He should be close enough to present a second challenge to the attacker should the No. 1 defender be beaten. Ideally, he should be close enough to dispossess the forward before he has regained his composure on the ball, therefore, denying him space in which to beat the No. 1 defender and time for him either to select a pass or balance himself to take on a covering player.

This distance may be influenced by the knowledge you have of the opponent. If he is inclined to rely on close control to beat his opponents then the supporting player may decide to cover closely. If, on the other hand, the opponent is known to rely almost entirely on change of pace to play the ball forward and accelerate past opponents, the No. 2 defender would be foolish to adopt a close supporting position where both defenders can be exposed by the speed of the attacker.

The whole concept of the No. 2 defender's role changes when we introduce his marking responsibil-

we looked at the covering role of No. 2 defenders, but now let us look to see how the picture changes when another attacker is introduced (Fig. 31).

If the covering player's positioning is not equally divided between his roles the attackers have an avenue to explore. For instance, if X2 marks X10 tightly in any of these situations X4 is vulnerable. On the other hand, if X2 moves too far behind X4 he leaves X10 with time to receive and exploit the space.

A game with three against three provides situations for players to experience the changing roles. In this practice it may be decided that a goal is scored if the ball can be stopped anywhere on the opponents' goal line without passing over the line. The area of the field of play must be large enough to enable frequent changes in the positions of the defenders. The pitch should be sufficiently wide to allow the team in possession space to stretch the defenders. Often an area the size of the penalty area is suitable.

In this exercise it is easy to identify the changing roles of the players and all six players will be required

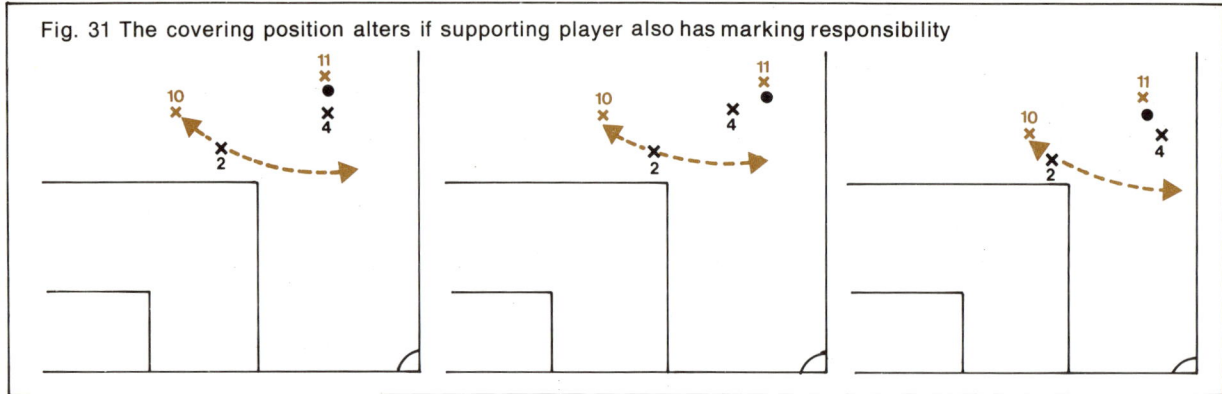

Fig. 31 The covering position alters if supporting player also has marking responsibility

to adopt the roles of challengers as well as those of covering players. The team losing the ball must decide instantly who will become the No. 1 defender and, indeed, this question must be answered by the defenders whenever a different opponent takes possession of the ball. Whenever a player closes down an opponent the other two should support the challenge. Both these players are, therefore, No. 2 defenders at this moment and either may be required to take on the role of the No. 1 defender if the ball is passed towards their opponent. When covering they should always be able to see the ball and the player that they are marking at the same time. If they find themselves in a position where this cannot be done they are very vulnerable, as besides being out of position, should a through ball be played, they cannot follow the movement of the opponent who is on the 'blind side'.

The team in possession should be encouraged to interchange positions to provide constant practice to their opponents in their marking and covering roles. In matches there may be times when even more than two players are performing covering duties, but their responsibilities still come under those of the No. 2 defenders.

The challenger and his supporting player(s) must work together and the covering player must provide information to assist the challenging player. One of the most common problems occurs when two attack-

ing players combine to play a 'wall pass'. When this is attempted in a two against two situation where one of the defenders has accepted the role of the No. 1 defender and his team mate has moved into a covering/ marking position (No. 2 defender), the tendency is for the challenging player to follow the ball rather than to turn the other way to keep with his man. This allows the attacker to gain a few precious metres. This is an instance when the supporting player should assess the problem and let his colleague know that a man for man situation exists so that he stays with his man. Once an understanding has been established regarding the balance between cover and marking in an even-sided game, players should be exposed to practices where the defending team is outnumbered by attackers. For instance, three players (plus a goalkeeper) defend the goal with four attackers trying to score. The width of the area should be sufficient to stretch the defenders, but not wide enough to make the practice unrealistic. The actual size of this area, and indeed all practice areas, will depend on the age and ability of the players. If you organise team practices do not continue with an area that is found to be too large for the players concerned. An adjustment only takes a few seconds!

In a practice of this kind the defenders must work together using the basic principles of the No. 1 and No. 2 defenders. They will need frequently to adjust their roles from challenger to covering player and vice versa, as well as continually being required to take up covering/marking positions. Despite being out-numbered it will be possible to achieve a high degree of success if the players work hard to delay the man on the ball providing time for the other two defenders to cover.

Additional players can, at the team leader's discretion, be added to both teams as the area is extended. One or two players positioned near to the halfway line provide the goalkeeper and defenders with a target for their clearances. These players will also enable the practice to flow as when they receive the ball they can play it in to the attackers. Forwards must be aware of the offside law and defenders should try to push the attackers back towards the halfway line following a clearance.

No. 3 defenders
My No. 3 defenders are those defending players away from the immediate challenge and who are too far away to provide the first line of cover to the No. 1 defender. It is these players who provide balance to the defence.

It is vital that all defenders are not drawn towards the ball. If this should happen the defence becomes lopsided and provides the opposition with a chance of changing the play to exploit the unguarded side of the defence. A balanced defence deploys its players in the best possible way to counteract the point of the attack, while at the same time being able to adjust quickly to respond to any change in the direction of the attack.

Therefore, the two main functions of the No. 3 defenders are to position themselves so that they are able to adjust a) to provide a third line of defence should both the challenger and covering player(s) be beaten – providing depth to the defence and b) to take on the role of the No. 1 or No. 2 defender should the point of attack be changed (Fig. 32).

Balancing players are usually at the back of the defence in a position where they can see the whole of the defence. Their responsibilities are divided by their

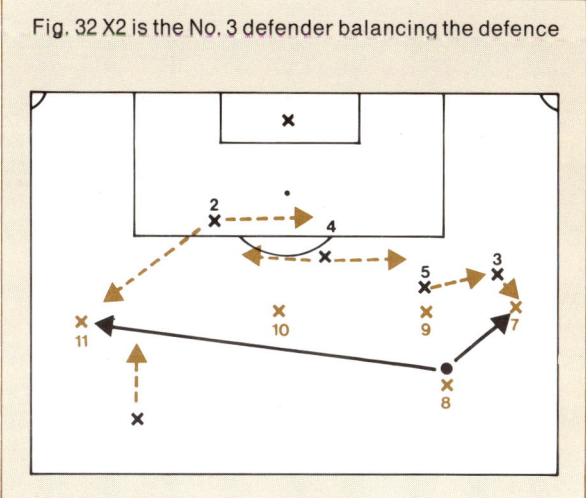

Fig. 32 X2 is the No. 3 defender balancing the defence

marking and balancing roles. One of the dangers is that they become too conscious of the problems surrounding the immediate attack and may fall into the trap of 'ball watching'. This is when players are so concerned with watching the ball that they lose sight of the positions and movement of other players. If you find yourself in the role of the No. 3 defender you must always find a position where you can see the ball and the man you are marking. This will avoid players moving up on your 'blind side'. Whenever you are the last defender on the opposite side to the ball (as X2 in Fig. 32) get into the habit of having a glance over your shoulder to check that the picture has not changed. This will serve as a double check to make sure that you are positioned between your man and the goal.

If the ball is played to an unmarked player on your side of the field a decision must be made quickly to decide who should take the responsibility to challenge. Communication between players is essential to stop two players committing themselves to the challenge. If you should take on the responsibility you must adjust quickly to adopt the role of the No. 1 defender. Can you intercept? If not, jockey and perhaps tackle! Should another player become the No. 1 defender then you should provide cover as a No. 2 defender.

One of the most difficult decisions a defence must make is to decide when it is safe to move upfield away from the defensive zone. When the defending team wins possession and starts to build an attack of its own it is straight forward because its players must move upfield to support the play, to avoid the team being 'stretched'. Players should endeavour to move forward and backwards as a unit to avoid large spaces being created between attackers and supporting players. This is good team tactics, but the decision becomes more difficult when the ball is only half cleared. The standard defensive play is for the defence to move upfield to compress the spaces available to the attackers. At the same time this may catch any forwards who do not respond offside when the ball is played forward. The decision for the defence to move out in this way is usually the decision of one of the No. 3 defenders. Once the decision has been made players must all respond to the call to move out. Any player who hesitates or stays can play the attackers 'on-side'. Often it is the balancing defender, who is the backman with farthest to move out who should take the responsibility to call the play, because he is in the best position to assess the situation.

When this situation occurs it requires the nearest defender to the attacker gaining possession to move in tightly to pressurise – in other words, to adopt the role of the No. 1 defender. Normally defences are square at this particular time and, therefore, it is essential that the challenger maintains his concentration and realises the importance of not being beaten by the forward. Occasionally skilful players can exploit defences in this way by pretending to pass the ball as a means of disguising an attempt to dribble through on their own. This is always a danger to the defence, as they create more space behind them for the forward to exploit with every metre that they advance.

Tackling

The main object of defensive play is to stop the opposition from scoring. The secondary function is to win possession of the ball. I have so far discussed the roles of individuals and groups of defenders in the overall defensive strategy but have not actually examined tackling.

The most disturbing feature when watching young players is the lack of restraint that is shown. When the opposition has possession of the ball its task of maintaining possession is made easier if we rush into challenges without having fully assessed the consequences. Good defenders follow the code governed by the defensive principles of play and exercise patience while looking for the chance to win the ball. The main problem in this respect is overcoming human nature. Players who class themselves as defenders usually enjoy the physical aspects of the game and must learn to control their desire to tackle. *Restraint* is the key word because unless players understand the dangers of thoughtlessly committing themselves to a challenge, they will never improve.

I have seen through experience that if players combine to close down the man in possession and provide support to the challenging player that there is every prospect of winning the ball without any tackle being made. Attackers placed in these circumstances often give the ball away through poor passing caused by the pressure exerted by defenders.

All players need to be aware of opportunities to win the ball and where tackling is concerned it can be broken down into two main areas. There are tackles where the object is purely to dispossess the man with the ball and others where you try to win possession for yourself. In both cases players need to possess courage and determination. There will be times when defenders have to commit themselves in desperate situations, where it is vital to make contact with the ball, purely to get the ball away from an opponent. Often a firm contact is required to play the ball far enough to allow time for the defence to regroup. On other occasions even the lightest of touches will be sufficient to play the ball into touch or towards a team mate. Faint-hearted players are a liability in such circumstances and this is often the main difference between attacking and defending players. At any level of play, forwards normally possess greater skill on the ball, which aids them in their creation of attacks, whereas defenders must have qualities of determination to test the skill of forwards. Players who have a high level of both become the better players in their respective standards of play.

In my opinion it is important for young players to understand the basic points of technique, but it is more important that they should understand when and where not to tackle. If you were to examine a full match and pay particular attention to the ball-winning ability of a team, you would see that possession is mostly regained through interception, with very few tackles winning the ball. Even in a man for man situation good defenders are able to force their opponent to make errors in control or dribbling so that the ball can be won without an actual tackle being made.

However, there are occasions where two players compete for possession both players having made contact with the ball at exactly the same time. When two players meet each other approaching the ball from opposite directions a *block tackle* usually occurs. Often too much emphasis is placed on describing this particular tackle giving the impression that it is a commonplace occurrence. In fact, I feel that these situations rarely occur, for usually one player is better placed than the other. In all tackles where two players play the ball at the same time the same principles should be applied.

Front block tackle

Once the decision has been made to tackle:
1 Place the standing foot as near to the side of the ball as possible
2 Adopt a position with the knees slightly bent – head over the ball
3 This sitting position will enable a firm contact on the ball to be made with the inside of the tackling foot.

Sliding tackle

Before you commit yourself to a *sliding tackle* be certain that you can reach behind the ball. Knowing this will enable you to keep your options open. At the last moment you can decide to kick the ball away from your opponent or to hook your foot around the ball in an attempt to win possession.

Courage is necessary to place a firm contact behind the ball. Anything less will be pushed aside by a more determined opponent. This applies equally to a *sliding tackle* where the inside or outside of an outstretched leg is concerned or to a *block tackle* where the inside of the foot makes contact with the ball. In tackles made from a standing position the centre of gravity of the body should be lowered to present a strong challenge, and this is the reason for the sitting position being adopted.

We have already discussed the responsibilities of challengers whose skill is assessed in knowing when they should commit themselves. Defenders should endeavour not to 'telegraph' their intention to tackle because this provides the man with the ball the chance to take avoiding action. The earlier defenders commit themselves to a tackle, the more time the opponent is given to assess the situation.

Remember: Don't force a confrontation in a man for man situation unless you have support from a covering player. *Don't* show your hand too early.

When you do decide to tackle you must be determined to win the ball. Association Football is a game which contains physical contact. This is an integral part of the game and all players must be prepared to accept such challenges. Some players, often the most skilful, cannot produce their best when faced by a strong tackling opponent. It is quite acceptable for defenders to test the courage of their opponents by tackling firmly as long as their challenges do not contravene the laws of the game. When clearances have to be made while under pressure there are a few

61

points to be remembered:

1 The farther the ball is cleared the more time is available for defences to re-organise
2 High clearances away from crowded penalty areas do not carry as much risk of being blocked as those equally hurried clearances below body height
3 Normally it is safer to clear to the wings than into the middle of the field of play, because not only are there usually fewer players in the wide areas (especially if the ball is cleared to the opposite side from the direction it came) but should it be controlled by an opponent the angle is less dangerous to a direct shot.

Some forward players move through their careers without ever coming to terms with the art of tackling. In fact, many forward players who are brave enough to accept the physical challenges of opponents seem reluctant to place their opponents under the same pressure when the opportunity arises. I always feel embarrassed for players who often find themselves with the chance to tackle, but who continually time their challenge so that they arrive just too late. This may seem difficult to understand, but I have known many forwards who fall into this category – perhaps it applies to you! The situation to which I refer is perhaps when the opposing goalkeeper throws the ball to his full back as the attacking player moves across to place him under pressure. Often it is possible to tell that the attacker will never block the clearance because although giving the impression that he has every intention of making a positive challenge it is easy to see him pacing his run to allow the full back just enough time to complete the clearance. The situation presents itself in several forms and in similar circumstances I like to see forward players who show sufficient determination genuinely to attempt to dispossess the defender.

Tracking down

Many goals result from the attacking players being allowed to run past defenders to the rear of the defence. Often apparently insignificant runs by forwards turn out to be very costly indeed for defenders. The initial move of the forward may not seem of too much importance because it may not be to support the immediate play. In these circumstances marking players sometimes become casual and fail to keep on the goal-side of their men, so that they are badly positioned when needed to present a telling challenge. On other occasions defenders are so concerned with their own particular opponent that they fail to realise the greater danger caused by an unmarked attacker moving past them. This often results in a numerical advantage to the attacking team at the back of the defence, where for instance a two against one situation can be fatal to the defence. A run of this type can also destroy a defence's cover because the covering player may be forced into marking the runner. In this way a crucial man for man situation at the back of the defence can spell danger, especially if, by good passing, the attackers can play the ball into this foremost attacker.

Do not bury your head in the sand and take the attitude that the runner is a team mate's problem. Defending requires players to work together and a fellow defender's problem is also your problem. Therefore, a decision must be taken quickly to enable you to take up the best position to safeguard the defence as a whole. The priority may call for you to leave your own man to move with this greater danger.

If an opponent is trying to run past you it may be possible to 'pass him on' to another defender. In other words you must communicate to a team mate to make sure that he will take responsibility for the opponent, leaving you to mark your own attacker or even move to close down the point of the attack.

Chapter 6 Principles of play: Attack

The basic concepts of Association Football are easy to understand and this is one of the great attractions of the game. However, books on football always seem to make the practical application appear simple. Nothing could be further from the truth! Having now discussed the defensive principles I hope that I have not given this impression. The many key factors that have been examined not only need to be understood, but must be practised to enable players to gain experience in making decisions in response to the ever-changing face of the opposition's attack.

We have established earlier that the side in possession of the ball is the attacking team so that when a team gains possession *all* players should regard themselves as attackers. This means that the players should combine to apply pressure onto the opponents' defence, in anticipation of scoring a goal.

Having seen how all defensive systems should be based on proven principles, we should look from an attacking viewpoint to discover how we can cause most concern to defences. The first priority is to become proficient in the principles of possession. We have previously discussed the many components that make up *control, pass* and *support,* and in effect have covered a great deal of the basics of attacking play in this way. However, if we understand the principles of defence we should look to examine the fundamental concepts of attacking play, which will test the practical capabilities of our opponents' defensive qualities.

Defences mainly feel at their most secure when they have 11 players between the ball and the goal. Teams may retain possession of the ball for some time, but will cause defences little concern unless they are able to play the ball forwards, past a defender and still maintain possession. Good defenders attempt to deny attackers the opportunity of playing the ball forwards and, consequently, defenders are happy to see the ball being played across the field in front of their defence. Every time we are able to play the ball forward successfully past an opponent we have achieved *penetration.*

For this to be achieved players should always look to play the ball forwards to a more advanced player where support can be provided, or where a man for man situation can be created. Support can be provided behind or ahead of the ball and can only be achieved if teams move forward and back as a unit. This avoids stretching the players and therefore isolating them. When gaining possession players should support any ball that is played forward. In addition to making players available for a pass, it reduces the space for your opponents to work in should they win possession.

If, on or before receiving a pass, you have assessed that the risks of losing the ball by playing it forward are too great, then you will require support behind or level with the ball. Young players must learn that it is sometimes better to play the ball back to supporting players rather than risk losing possession. Often this is the only way to maintain possession for your team and the best positive backward passes are those which open up an opportunity to play the ball forward to a more advanced player. Passes that are played back without any consideration to the merits of going forward are often negative.

Practice

To encourage players in developing this awareness of going forward a small-sided practice can be set up as follows. In a small-sided game of six-or eight-a-side, each team should nominate a target man. The object of the game is for the players to look to see if they can pass the ball to their target man. To encourage players to pick him out with a pass, award a point every time his team mates successfully bring him into the game and two points for a goal being scored. The practice educates players to increase their awareness of the positions of team mates and opponents and this assists them in selecting the pass. It is not sufficient just to hit the target player for the quality of pass must enable him to maintain possession for the team.

In the aforementioned practice the target man must work to be available to receive passes and should constantly be seeking positions where he can show for

63

the pass. In games with eight against eight it may be preferred to introduce an additional target player so that the two players can work together, which will make the practice so much more realistic.

Attacking principles are impossible to isolate for *penetration* cannot be achieved unless players work to break down other defensive principles. For instance, if we know that defences feel secure when several players gather between the ball and the goal, we should endeavour to employ tactics to draw defenders away from their goal. If one or more players can be enticed away from the vital area in front of goal, it provides space for our attackers to exploit. Teams capable of drawing players away from this concentration of defenders most often look to create *width* in attack. This entails players looking for opportunities to receive the ball near to the touch lines, where a defender must come if he wishes to stop progress being made. This tactic has the effect of stretching defences from side to side. *Width* does not necessarily mean the use of wingers, for even in teams that have no wide-playing forwards, other players should work to provide *width*.

In the diagram we can see X7 moving in-field. The full back X2 has seen the space being created and has moved forward to form an overlap, at the same time creating *width* (Fig. 33).

The ball can either be played from X7 into the feet of X8 or X9, who can exploit the *width* available by passing to X2. This must help in breaking the *concentration* of defenders in the main scoring area.

Width should also be related to the area of play. For instance, in a two against one situation in any area of the pitch, the two attacking players must move wide enough apart to ensure that the defender cannot mark both players. Only then can one player commit the defender, so that he is unable to recover once the pass has been made. In Fig. 34 the defender is able to mark two players. In Fig. 35 they are using the width available to great advantage.

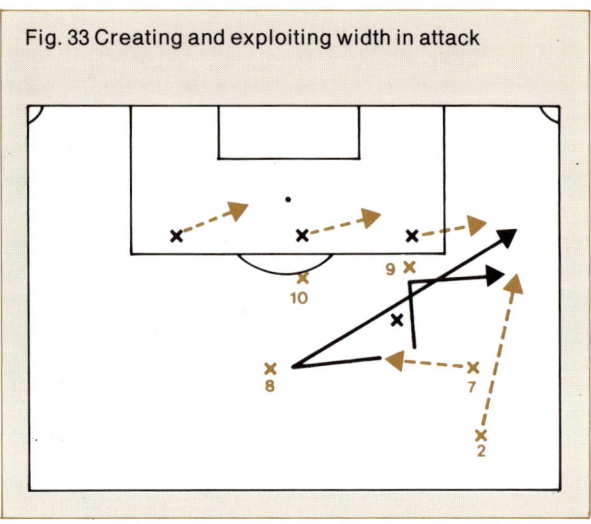

Fig. 33 Creating and exploiting width in attack

Small-sided games are an ideal way of working for an understanding of the principles of play. Players who stay within the same area cause little problem, whereas players who are continually interchanging positions to create *width* make it possible for attacks to stretch defences from side to side.

Active players supply *mobility* to the attack, which enables *penetration* to be achieved. Static players are easy to mark, but players who are prepared continually to move around seeking to join in the attacking play are constantly posing problems to defenders.

I remember a piece of advice that was given to me when I was 18 years old. It came during the half-time interval of a match when I was playing against an experienced professional central defender. I had worked hard, but had failed to make any impression and I was grateful for my team mate's encouragement. He said that I had two alternatives, I could either concede defeat and stop trying, or I could be determined to help the overall team performance by working even harder. He explained that the game was about making decisions. Even good players occasionally make the wrong decision, so if I was prepared to

Fig. 34 Forwards are too close, giving defender a chance to win possession

Fig. 35 Now with the forwards wider apart the defender has little chance

Another brilliant save by Peter Shilton

keep competing by showing for the ball and asking questions of my opponent, it may result in him making an error from which our team could benefit. Giving up would not test his ability at all. I am pleased to say that his advice paid dividends.

There are bound to be games when our opposite number seems invincible, but attackers should always remember that although they may lose the overall individual contest they only need one chance to make a vital contribution to the match. I can recall many matches when I made the headlines in the match reports through scoring the vital goal, when I knew that my overall performance was below par.

Any controlled run without the ball, particularly those to the back of defences, or which cause an interchange of positions, will assist in causing confusion to defenders. Questions will be asked and defenders must immediately come up with the correct decisions. Any slight hesitation may be sufficient for the attack to take full advantage.

I hope you can appreciate the contribution that *width* and *mobility* demand from players if *penetration* is to be achieved. Always remember the importance of *control, pass* and *support* in attacking play, which should not be forgotten.

Let us now consider some practices which help in understanding the principles of attack while testing the players' ability.

1   Possession cannot be maintained unless players provide support to the man on the ball. So let us look at a simple practice to encourage players to make themselves available to receive a pass. In a small-sided game make it a condition that a forward pass must be followed by a backward pass, and so on. The only time the sequence can be broken is if the man in possession decides to try to score. Players must be mobile continually to support both in front and behind the ball. It is also a good practice for forwards who, when unable to go forward, must hold on to the ball while under pressure from an opponent, to allow time for players to support behind the ball. Once again, players should play as if they are permitted only two touches of the ball, even though this condition has not been made.

2   *Control, pass and support* can be encouraged if we offer points to the two teams of eight or so players. If a point is given every time a team strings together an agreed number of consecutive passes (10 for good performers) it will give an incentive to players to produce a high quality of passing. Two points could be awarded for any goal that is scored with three points if the goal is scored with a first touch on the ball. This practice will enable teams to show patience in building an attack, which will develop confidence in keeping possession of the ball until an opportunity arises to strike for goal. Therefore, the principles of supporting play and *width* and *mobility* will be seen in their contribution to achieving *penetration*.

3   A two touch practice in a two-sided game of eight players enables a practice with a high transfer value to be organised. The area that I use is that bounded by the edge of the penalty area, the half-way line and the two touch lines.
A goal is scored if the ball is stopped on the touch line (without passing over it). The fact that the goal line is about 23 metres long provides opportunities for mobile players to penetrate. Three touches are only allowed when the third touch stops the ball on the line. Players can be encouraged to play to front players and the fact that only two touches are allowed makes players support the man with the ball. If each player is given an opponent to mark it develops an awareness and helps players to understand the importance of keeping the ball and opponent in view.

4   All players are inclined to follow the ball, particularly young players. This practice allows plenty of realistic work to be accomplished in using space. Divide the pitch down the middle with markers between the penalty areas and produce

67

two evenly numbered teams on one half of the pitch. The teams should consist of a goalkeeper, two defenders, two midfield players and two attackers. Encourage players to use the full space available. There are no offsides so front players can push up as far as possible. The practice enables squads of teams to confront realistic situations as the time and distance between players is realistic. Playing in this manner allows members of a squad to play in their correct position so that patterns of play can be established. The game can be programmed further to force players to find their target men and if players can be restricted to play in their positional areas the game is very realistic. For those responsible for clubs with two teams it is possible to have the same practice on both sides of the field using 28 to 32 players in all. If this is tried the goalkeepers occasionally have to cope with two shots at the same time. This is a rare occurrence, but in any case, goalkeepers must keep alert. Later the two individual practices can be combined by using one ball and restricting players to stay on their own side of the dividing line. Players keep the same positions and are able to pass the ball across the dividing line to bring the other players into play. The goalkeepers must feed the ball back into play by clearing to the opposite side from the direction of the last attack. The game becomes a fluid enjoyable exercise with many permutations possible.

How can we encourage mobility? For players to be capable of the physical aspects of Association Football they must be fit enough to carry out the many specific demands that the game makes. Therefore, mobility must come under the umbrella of fitness, which will be mentioned later. Players must understand how active players can destroy defences, for this will act as an incentive.

Movement off the ball

If problems are to be posed to the opposition, passing must be made as unpredictable as possible. The more options that are made for the passer the more difficult it is for the defending side to read how play will develop. One way of achieving this aim is for players to move into positions to receive the ball early. This means that supporting players should be moving before the ball reaches the receiver. Poor teams only assess each situation after the ball reaches the receiving player and this makes the chances of producing a sequence of passes impossible.

Players running off the ball as the ball is in flight to a team mate provide the chance of playing an early ball to alter the point of attack quickly. If this can be followed on in the same way it must cause concern to the defending team. On the other hand the team that only moves to support after a man gains possession has little chance of causing a threat to its opponents.

One of the main problems is to encourage players who have passed the ball to support. The tendency is to watch and admire the pass and players need constantly to be aware of their contribution off the ball. Having passed the ball players should move into a supporting position and be ready to regain possession. This is illustrated in a standard move known as 'the third man run'. The move involves a player making a forward run while two team mates set up the move (Fig. 36). X2 having received the ball works a 'setting-up' pass to X3. On receiving the ball back from X3, who has moved towards the ball (which may help to create space by dragging X4 with him) he is now able to play the ball forward to meet the run of X1. This well used ploy is easily understood by average players and is not too difficult to integrate into a team's play.

It is necessary to have mobile players even when there is a numerical advantage in the attackers' favour, but obviously it is even more important when the attackers are outnumbered by defenders. I like to use lopsided practices to force the outnumbered forwards to work hard to achieve success. If we play into a goal with four forwards competing against five defenders, the attackers will be made to work if they are to succeed in causing problems.

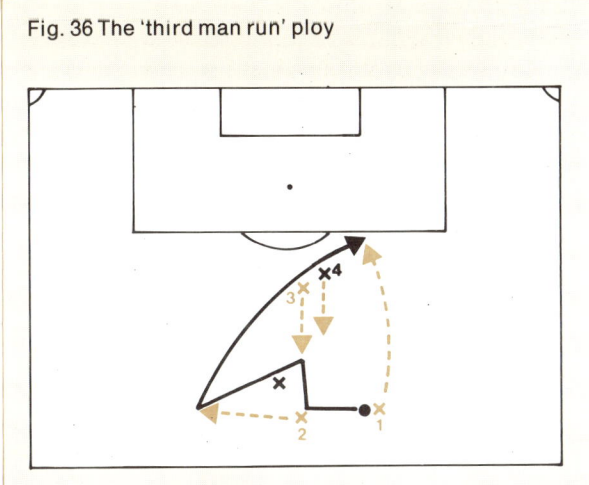

Fig. 36 The 'third man run' ploy

In this practice forward players will be compelled to move to find space. The forwards are supported by a player whose role is purely to feed the ball into the attacks and also to act as a target for the defenders when they gain possession. In this way the practice can flow in a realistic manner. Mobility of players enables width to be created and also instant decisions are asked from defenders to decide who should mark the runner. When dealing with the defensive principles we looked at the difficulties caused by players who make runs across defenders and to the back of the defence. Now is the chance to try to catch the defenders out. The quality of control, pass and support must be good and the players should be looking to select the pass that will pick out a one against one situation, particularly at the back of the defence.

In the attacking third of the pitch, players should be encouraged to express their flair and natural ability by dribbling past opponents or by performing skills requiring a high level of technique such as volleys or overhead kicks. Coaches should inspire forward players to try the unexpected around the penalty area where most of these attempts to produce a chance to score will be unsuccessful, but goals usually derive from these flashes of improvisation that do succeed.

Dribbling

One of the most difficult skills to acquire is the ability to move the ball while keeping it under control. It is one of the most spectacular sights in football. Everyone enjoys watching a skilful ball player who has the ability to take the ball past defenders. It is an individual skill which players should develop into their own style and coaches should encourage players to cultivate a confidence on the ball.

We have already discussed acquiring touch and this area of the game is where players who have a feel for the ball will be at an advantage. When the ball has been controlled a player must decide on his next course of action. On assessing the conditions that he finds himself in he may decide to move with the ball rather than pass to another player. Sometimes he will need to keep the ball close, whereas in others he may be able to play the ball into a safe space and follow quickly after it. Whatever the situation, the touch on the ball must be appropriate.

Players should be encouraged to play the ball with both the inside and outside of the feet during training because this helps in keeping balance, as the ball can be played simply without any awkward movement. There have been and always will be good players who are very 'one footed'. Although there will be exceptions the majority of players who strongly favour a particular foot are easier to read than 'two footed' players. This is another incentive for players to practise using both feet; even the best one-sided players would have been better had they improved their ability on the weaker side. Often it boils down to confidence and this can only be attained in practice conditions.

One of the features of dribbling is the *change of pace* that occurs. Opponents can be deceived by sudden starts and stops, so time can be productively spent in working alone with a football until control can be comfortably maintained during these movements. Sometimes players need to move quickly and other times at a walking pace. It is the ability to change

69

pace while maintaining control of the ball which is the difference between good and bad ball players. Besides changes of pace, the ability to *change direction* is another asset and when these features are combined to good effect it provides tremendous problems for defenders.

Initially practices should allow players to work for confidence on the ball. There is no need to provide challenging players too early until beginners can manoeuvre the ball reasonably well. A good basic practice for beginners can be set up by providing several players with a football and asking them all to stay within an area which can be varied as required. The players should then move around the area maintaining control of the ball while avoiding collisions with the other players.

Various conditions can be made to ensure that the players gain practice in the many features of dribbling. The coach can issue various instructions to test the abilities of the players. The players will, for instance, be called upon to stop and start while being encouraged to accelerate into spaces as they appear.

When in control of the ball, players should try to widen their vision so that the decision can be made to release the ball at the correct time to a colleague in a better position. It is the ability to keep good vision that helps in deciding when to dribble and when to pass. Players should try to acquire the habit of lifting their head to keep abreast with the ever-changing picture.

The most difficult aspect is taking the ball past defenders. The man on the ball must try to disguise his intentions. Often this is achieved by feinting to move one way, to transfer the opponent's weight to one side before changing direction to move the opposite way (Fig. 37). Plenty of movement of ball and body makes it difficult for defenders to weigh up the situation. While speed is a useful quality it is not only the fastest runners who can take the ball past opponents. Players who can disguise their intentions and are able to 'wrong foot' their opposite number can gain a few metres advantage without necessarily being fast movers. The asset that really needs to be combined with disguise is change of pace. Players who

Fig. 37A Feinting movements

Fig. 37B Now accelerate past your opponent

Unbelievable height and power by Cyril Regis

can move slowly before 'exploding' past defenders, or when running can change into a lower gear to produce a sudden extra metre of space will always be valuable to a team. This emphasises the need for players to practise moving with the ball, with sudden starts, stops and changes of direction, and will assist in creating the extra space required to shoot or pass to a team mate.

There are no hard and fast rules, but players will naturally develop their own style using movements that they find most natural. Individual skills that can exploit an opponent win matches, particularly in the attacking third of the pitch. It is within this area that attacking space is scarce and players should be encouraged to commit defenders. Players should be encouraged in this area of the pitch, for success will not be achieved on every occasion, but the rewards for an occasional success can be high. Players will develop their own style by practising in one to one situations. An example of a type of competitive game to allow such practice would be to number the players and then on calling out two numbers the appropriate players move quickly to compete for possession of the ball. The man winning possession then attempts to bypass his opponent to reach a given target. This game can provide an enjoyable competition whether indoors or outside.

A variation could be to play the ball into one of the players who has a challenger behind him. This will provide the chance to practise turning with the ball to face the defender and also in 'screening' the ball from challengers. When screening the ball it is important to keep the ball as far away from the opponent as possible. This can best be done by avoiding being square to the challenger by turning one shoulder towards the opponent (Fig. 38). Besides allowing the ball to be kept away from your opponent this position improves your vision at the same time, allowing you to turn in either direction.

Fig. 38A When screening, do not stand square with ball

Fig. 38B Keep ball away from opponent, turn sideways

The basics of screening can also be experienced in the earlier practice when several players are employed in controlling footballs in a confined area. A challenger can be introduced into the area with the object of winning possession of a ball. Those in possession are forced to use the skills of dribbling to prevent their ball from being taken. Not the least skill is that of keeping the body between the ball and the opponent. When the challenger wins possession of a football the dispossessed player then seeks to win possession from another player.

Defences are placed at a disadvantage if the attackers can gain possession of the ball anywhere on the goal-line because when the ball is crossed it comes on to forwards and away from defenders. In these circumstances it is more difficult for defenders to mark their opposite numbers and see the ball at the same time, so the attackers have the opportunity to gain an advantage by moving on to the blind side or to gain the vital metre of space by accelerating to meet the ball at the near post. The fact that an attacker has managed to reach the goal-line makes it necessary for a defender to move to offer a challenge, leaving an attacker unmarked.

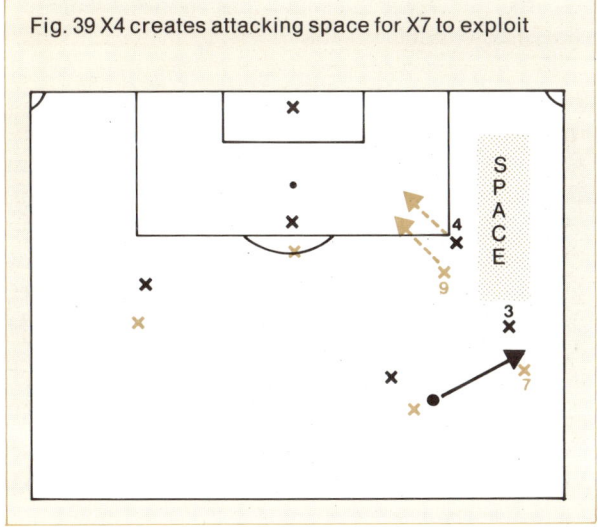

Fig. 39 X4 creates attacking space for X7 to exploit

In these circumstances other players should recognise situations where a quick player has an opportunity to test his marker. There is nothing worse than for a rare one to one opportunity to arise only to see another attacker run behind the defender, thus destroying the space. In Fig. 39, X7 has a chance to use his pace as there is space for him to attack behind X3. In these circumstances X9 should move away in an attempt to keep X4 from moving behind X3, to provide cover that he desperately needs.

Improvisation can be practised in the following routine: two teams of three players move into the penalty area, together with a goalkeeper. A server stands on the edge of the area with as many footballs as possible. Other players awaiting their turn should surround the playing area to feed the balls back to the server. The conditions of the game are that the player who gains possession when a ball is played in can only attempt to score. He is not permitted to pass to his team mates. The other team must attempt to stop him shooting and as soon as any of the other five players gain possession they can only try to score – not to pass. As soon as the ball leaves the area another ball can be played in. Players should be urged to create a shooting chance by making space with individual flair. Perhaps two goals can be awarded for any goal that is scored with a first touch contact on the ball. This may encourage players to volley, head or spin to strike the ball goalwards. Alert players will cash in on rebounds from the other attackers, goalkeeper or woodwork, which will create the type of chances that occur in real match situations. The server can vary the way he feeds the ball into the area. On occasions picking out a player in space to encourage dribbling or perhaps tossing a ball to a player in a tight situation where a first touch volley or header may pay dividends.

Although the practices have been to concentrate on principles of attack, they could all be used for defenders to practise the defensive principles.

73

Chapter 7 **Shooting**

The net result

Having examined the principles of attack we should now look at the problem of actually putting the ball into the net. To my mind this is the most important aspect of the game because the essence of football is about players having the ability to create and accept chances to score. We often see opportunities to shoot created but not accepted because the player has lacked confidence, as the fear of missing has been stronger than the belief in the ability to score. Coaches should try to dispel this fear and encourage players to look for and accept the chances when they arise.

Goal-scorers have come to terms with the fact that scoring is a matter of percentages because for every shot that results in a goal many more are unsuccessful. Sometimes the weakest effort finishes in the back of the net whereas a powerfully struck shot is saved. What is certain is that all goals, whether they are scored from 30 metres or 30 centimetres, count the same and that a tamely hit shot on target has a chance to score where a fierce drive that is just too high or wide will never score, unless it is deflected into goal.

Contact

If accuracy is the number one priority, there is a need for a correct contact on the ball and for players to understand the effect that the various contacts have on the flight of the ball. Contact is usually made with a moving ball and so initially time should be spent dealing with the many contacts to improve the technique of each. In a match a competitive contact requires a split second decision to shoot and often a shot needs to be improvised because there is no time to move into a 'posed' position. It is in these circumstances that an inbuilt knowledge of the mechanics of kicking a ball will be an advantage. Therefore, players should not only practise shooting by striking balls in their own time, but should experience situations when reflex shots are necessary.

Shooting covers a wide subject as it entails every type of shot from the instep drive at long distances as well as to the toe-end shots from near the goal-line. In the World Cup Finals we saw many spectacular goals that were scored from 25 to 30 metres or more from goal. From this distance, only players who have perfected their technique will trouble goalkeepers. Not only are they able to place tremendous power into the shot (caused by the quick straightening action of the knee), but they also have developed the ability to 'bend' the ball, by striking it just off-centre. Players who attempt to score from such distances must have tremendous confidence in their ability for not only are the chances of scoring low, but in many cases the players in supporting positions have been ignored. The factor from the World Cup that most interested me was that when the shots from this range were unsuccessful it was noticeable that other players did not chastise the shooter. Obviously they realised the particular talent that the player possessed and were willing to encourage him rather than destroy his confidence.

Practices

When shooting we sometimes have the chance to assess the situation before selecting a particular type of shot, but mostly we are simply concerned with making contact with the ball in an effort to send it towards the target. I believe that shooting practices should be conducted in and around the penalty area so that players, who often do not have time to look for the goal, develop a natural awareness of the targets in relation to their own position. Even players with their backs to goal will be able quickly to assess the angle to goal from their position in relation to the penalty spot or corner of the goal areas.

The practice on page 73 dealing with improvisation is a useful game to provide shooting practice where players have little time to select their shot.

At one of my professional clubs I remember a chart being made to show the position from where all the goals both for and against were scored. This chart took the form of a large pitch where a dot was placed to illustrate the point from where each scoring shot was made. A small number of dots showed that

Trevor Francis of England displaying the exciting skills which make him such a favourite

some goals were scored from long distances, but the most distinctive feature was that the vast majority were scored from within the goal-area, where the physical contact is at its most intense. Most of the goals from this distance are scored by a one touch contact where the scorer has been brave and quick enough to be first to the ball. So, if you are a striker, try to look for opportunities to support the attack of other forwards by running into the goal-area and be prepared to follow in other players' shots in the hope of capitalising on a rebound from the goalkeeper or woodwork.

Low shots and shots to the far post

There are occasions when players do have time to select a particular shot and are able to aim for a particular part of the goal, so we should consider how we can cause most concern to the goalkeeper. All players, and particularly those of you who are forwards, should understand that low shots are more likely to be difficult to save than shots in the air. We have already discussed that goal scoring is a matter of percentages and I am certain that a goalkeeper who makes a spectacular save from a shot in the air would be more likely consistently to save that type of shot rather than a less powerful shot along the ground.

So remember that goalkeepers have less difficulty in moving their hands to save high shots, because they have less distance to move than when trying to save low shots. Bending takes longer than stretching and all low shots require the body as well as the arms to be moved.

Goalkeepers often make saves with their legs and body as well as with their hands. Shots that are struck firmly from close range require goalkeepers to make reflex saves. It is far easier to adjust hands quickly than to move the legs. Even a shot which is close enough to brush past the goalkeeper's leg may be impossible to save if his weight is on that leg. Even when you are in a situation where you do not have time to aim for a particular part of the goal you can at least be conscious of trying to keep the ball low.

It is said that low shots to the far post are most difficult to save and I am sure that in general this is true. However, it would be difficult to sell this idea to a player who had scored with a high shot to the near post, but who had also beaten the goalkeeper with a low shot to the far post only to see a full back recover to clear the ball from the line! Really the answer to this lies in the selection of the shot, for no two situations are exactly the same. Shooting low to the far post certainly presents a goalkeeper with difficulties because the ball is moving away and is therefore more difficult to hold. Often goals are scored by players capitalising on rebounds in these circumstances. It is probably true to say that when the goalkeeper is perfectly positioned he has more difficulty in saving shots that are low and to the far post.

Composure

It is strange how the temperament of individual players can vary depending on the area of the field in which they find themselves. Defenders are often unflappable in the defensive third, but become tense when in the attacking zone. Good strikers are those who stay calm in and around the penalty area; this allows them to concentrate on the job in hand. This composure is not easily developed, but we can help to improve it if we understand that the essential requirement is awareness. This can only be achieved if, when you have time, you lift your head.

This is particularly so when you are clear of the defence with only the goalkeeper to beat. In these circumstances concentrate on the touch on the ball so that you do not over-play it, making it easy for the goalkeeper to dispossess you. If you lift your head you will be aware of the advancing goalkeeper, which will help you decide either to attempt to beat him with a shot or to dribble past him.

The chip shot

If you decide to go around the goalkeeper, try to disguise your intentions and remember to play the ball far enough past, or away from him, to make it impossible for him to dive onto it. These situations always look easy, but never are. If the goalkeeper's angles are poor, it may allow you to decide to shoot, so try to keep the ball low. One of the most difficult skills to perform is a chip shot which is played if the goalkeeper has left his line too early, leaving a large space behind him. It is extremely difficult to chip a ball that is already moving in the direction of the intended shot, so try to move the ball slightly away from the line to goal and towards the shooting foot which will increase the chances of success.

The scorers

Shooting is not just one skill for it requires players to be proficient in a variety of circumstances. Good strikers have developed a high level of ability in the many requirements of the goal-scorer and you young players should try to adopt the particular strengths of the top players. I personally enjoy the competitiveness and agility of Kevin Keegan, the composure of Trevor Francis, the strength and quickness of Kenny Dalglish and the turning ability of Alan Curtis.

All these players have proven themselves as consistent goal-scorers in the past, but one thing is certain: none of these players converts every chance that comes his way. They all occasionally miss chances, some comparatively simple, but they still possess enough character to look eagerly for the next opportunity.

Practices

The primary objective is to be able to strike the ball cleanly, preferably with both feet. Build up your confidence by practising with a colleague, or against a rebound surface, until you can drive a ball powerfully, keeping the ball low – knee and head over the ball. Can you bend the ball? At first reduce the power of the kick and see if you can make the ball curve in flight by using the inside and outside of both feet.

1   Make a small goal and position yourself with colleagues about 20 metres on each side of the goal and practise playing the ball through the target –

remember, accuracy before power.

2   A practice to encourage a good first-time low drive would be to form players into a circle and simply ask them to drive the ball across the circle. Players receiving the ball control it and lay it off to a neighbour for him to drive the ball with his first touch.

3   A group of players line up 18 metres from the goal line at the corner of the penalty area, with a similar number in the centre circle, where the footballs are gathered. As an attacker leaves the centre circle with a ball, in an attempt to score past the goalkeeper, a defender moves forward to make his task more difficult. The defending player tries to prevent the attacker from scoring by following the principles of the No. 1 defender. (The players then return to the opposite group as this will provide practice in attack and defence.) The practice can be made more demanding for the attackers if instead of starting with a ball, they are made to control the ball that is served into them so that they must work quickly to gain possession before the defender.

4   Make a goal and position 3 to 4 players on each side. Challenge the players to beat the goalkeeper with a first time drive. If they are unable to shoot first time, they should control the ball and then play it to a colleague for him to shoot first time. Players can be conditioned to two touches only and should be encouraged to compete against the opposite team. The game may be conditioned further by positioning a player approximately 10 metres in front of goal. The other players can now select to play passes into him, for him to lay the ball off for a shot. Divide an area into three and position two attackers to one defender in each of the attacking areas. Two players compete against two in midfield. Players are restricted to their own areas and the game can be conditioned to limit the attackers to two touches to ensure that they work hard to score.

Chapter 8 Set plays

Free kicks, corners and throw-ins have had an increasingly important influence on the outcome of matches, as it has been established that in the region of 40 per cent of goals derive from these particular re-starts. Many players obviously do not recognise the value of such situations for they consistently fail to apply sufficient concentration to them, irrespective of whether they are for or against their team.

There is nothing worse than seeing a team, which has worked hard to exert pressure on the opponents' goal, being awarded a corner or a free kick in an attacking position, only to see the corner played directly behind for a goalkick or the shot sail harmlessly over the bar. Equally disappointing is to witness the defending side failing to mark attackers at a throw-in, or being caught off-guard by a quickly taken free kick which results in a goal being scored. So let us look at these set plays from both an attacking and defending point of view.

Free kicks
Attacking thoughts
When we first think of free kicks to our own team we most likely think of positions in the attacking third of the pitch. We should not forget that the majority of free kicks occur in the other areas of the field. The objectives, when taking a free kick, should be the same as when we are in possession during free play. The difference is that unlike in free play, opposing players should be 10 metres from the ball and, therefore, there is little pressure on the man taking the kick. If you are responsible for taking the kick you must decide between a safe pass to retain possession and perhaps a pass where the chances of losing possession are greater but the reward for success is a strike for goal. The longer you delay in taking the kick the more time the opposition have to mark tightly and to deny passing opportunities.

Other players should concentrate at such times and be aware of the importance of not being distracted because if you are able quickly to bring the ball into play by safely passing to an alert colleague, you may be able to catch the opposition off-guard. Often players of both teams become distracted when the referee's whistle signifies a free kick and this is the time when two players can combine to expose the lack of concentration of their opponents.

If there is a delay before the kick is taken it may be impossible to play a simple pass to an unmarked team mate. In these circumstances a longer pass may be decided upon, but the selection of the pass will depend on the situation at the time. It may be possible to play the ball into the strikers for an attempted header at goal, but whatever the decision everything should be done to make sure that a good contact is made on the ball.

When watching inexperienced players, it is noticeable that they often take the free kick without knowing exactly what they are trying to achieve. The ball is kicked towards an area without fully considering the objective when a little thought can provide the incentive to produce a more accurate free kick. This is particularly noticeable in windy conditions.

Windy conditions
When taking a free kick where the wind will affect the flight of the ball I believe you should take a few seconds to assess the amount of deviation that will occur. Then concentrate on aiming the kick towards a selected point allowing the conditions to move the ball to the desired target. If, for instance, the free kick is 30 metres from goal and near to the touch line and the objective is an area 10 metres out from the far post, it may be necessary to drive the ball firmly as if intending to hit the top of the near post, allowing the oncoming wind to do the rest. The power of the kick also needs to be calculated as it is obvious that the wind will affect the ball more as its pace decreases.

Unfortunately, the majority of young players seem to disregard the conditions and very few concentrate sufficiently in assessing the direction and

A characteristic picture of England's Trevor Brooking delivering another accurate cross

power needed to combat windy days. Sometimes it is useful to wait a few seconds to see if the wind momentarily drops in strength.

Although these remarks have been linked to free kick situations players should always relate conditions to their game throughout the whole 90 minutes. Set plays do provide more time for you to assess the wind and it disappoints me to see the flight of the ball being directed towards the target from the moment the ball leaves the boot when no allowance has been made for wind strength.

The placing of the ball can be vital for often I see players drop the ball, allow it to stop and then take the free kick. When a ball is left to roll it invariably comes to rest in a hollow, whereas accuracy is more likely to be achieved if the ball is 'teed' up.

Making a decision

So remember that the opportunity to take a free kick quickly is more likely to occur in the middle and defensive third of the pitch, where the opposition may show a lack of urgency. If it is impossible to play the ball quickly then take your time to make sure that the ball is placed to your advantage, and then *think* about the situation before playing the ball accurately.

Free kicks in and around the penalty area provide an opportunity to strike for goal. Once again, look for opportunities to catch the defence off-guard by a quickly taken kick, although defences are usually more alert in these situations.

If the opposition has an opportunity to prepare its defence we have two alternatives. We can decide to perform a pre-arranged move to open up a better opportunity to score or take a direct shot at goal. If an indirect free kick has been awarded the ball will obviously have to be played to a supporting player before a shot can be taken. We all have our favourite moves, designed to mislead the opposition, but I do not intend to examine any individual plan. The least complicated are the best as there are fewer factors to go wrong and it is easier for players to understand their roles.

Too many pre-planned set plays fail disastrously because players are uncertain of their part. Players, for some reason, do not concentrate in practice sessions as they should when rehearsing set plays. Make sure you understand your contribution.

Teams should play to their strengths in these circumstances. If your side contains a player who has the ability to 'bend' powerful shots then obviously it would be sensible to allow him to take the kicks. Make sure that your team gives the responsibility to the player most capable of either shooting or passing accurately.

It is noticeable that foreign teams rarely work a rehearsed free kick, for almost invariably they attempt a shot at goal. I am sure that they practise bending the ball far more than British players and are, therefore, better equipped in this department. During my playing career I played in many matches in other countries and there were numerous times when we complained to the referee that the ball was too soft. These complaints resulted in the referee pushing his thumbs into the ball before dismissing our complaint. This was one theory why continental sides always seemed to be able to curve the ball in flight, due to the foot being able to depress the surface of the ball on impact. The pressure of the ball has now been reduced in Britain so we can no longer use the same excuse. So, try to introduce this ability into your play for it will enable you also to bend the ball towards and away from goal when taking corners and free kicks, which always produce problems for defenders.

Defensive thoughts

Too many players lose their concentration when a free kick is given against their team. Players are, unfortunately, inclined to dispute the decision or take their attention away from the ball. This can be fatal should the opponents play the ball quickly. The first lesson is to make sure that you are aware of this weakness so that you mark up quickly. It is normal to place a man 10 metres from the ball between the ball and the goal. He will be looking to close down any short pass, at the same time restricting any direct route to goal. In addition, his presence may cause a distraction to the kicker should he decide to play a long pass to another attacker in the direction of the goal.

The situation becomes more critical with free kicks from in and around the penalty area. As soon as a kick has been awarded it is the goalkeeper's responsibility to decide if he requires a wall to be formed and, if so, how many players should form the wall. The wall should be formed quickly and, therefore, to avoid any delay players should know when they are needed to make up the required number.

Opinions about which players should form the wall vary and may depend on the abilities and physique of the players. Some teams prefer to keep as many defenders as possible out of the wall so that they are available to mark opponents. Most would agree that central defenders, who are usually good headers of the ball, should not form the wall. There is no one correct system and it is a matter for each team to decide the system that is best suited to its players.

Whatever system is used, I feel that it must have the approval of the goalkeeper, who is ultimately responsible for stopping the ball entering the goal. One of the problems that I have encountered is that goalkeepers like to line the wall up themselves, but this takes them behind the wall where they cannot see the ball. I have seen goalkeepers caught in an unsighted position lining up the wall as the ball has been kicked into the unguarded side of the goal. For this reason I like to see an outfield player directing the wall into the correct position. For this to meet with the goalkeeper's approval time should be spent to make sure that the goalkeeper has clearly shown the outfield players where, in relation to the near post, he requires the wall. Only then will he have confidence that the wall is sound. The goalkeeper is then responsible for covering the shot to the unguarded area from where he can see the ball. He should also be able to save any shot that moves over the wall to the unguarded side of the goal.

I personally believe that the important factors are that the system should be designed for the players clearly to understand their contribution so that the wall is formed quickly. Therefore, I work in the following way:

1   As soon as the free kick is awarded the goalkeeper should clearly call the number of players that are required in the wall

2   The full back on the same side of the pitch from where the kick has been given, immediately moves to a position between the ball and the near post

3   His position is adjusted by a forward player who moves behind the ball from where he can, by signals, adjust the full back's position

4   Other players required in the wall, while encouraged by the full back, move quickly to join the inside of the wall to form a solid barrier.

I like to use midfield players to form the remainder of the wall and they should know their responsibilities before the game, so that as soon as the goalkeeper calls, for example, 'Three in the wall!' two players immediately join the full back concerned.

It does not matter how far behind the ball the forward is who lines up the full back, as long as he moves to a position where the ball is in line with the post. Once on this 'line' he can be moving back towards the free kick, ready to defend, while at the same time signalling the full back to the correct position.

By this method only one man needs to be positioned for other players simply join him. Complete walls, say of four players, are always awkward to adjust because they rarely respond as one unit to signals. When lining up the 'anchor man' the forward concerned should make sure that at least two thirds of the full back's body is outside the line of the post to prohibit opponents from swerving the ball around the outside of the wall.

81

Goalkeepers need to practise defending at free kicks in this vital area to determine the number of players required in the wall in relation to the angle of the free kick (Fig. 40). It will probably work out as follows:

A For free kicks around the arc outside the penalty area four or possibly five players

B Between the arc and the corner of the penalty area three or four players

C From the sides of the penalty area one to three players.

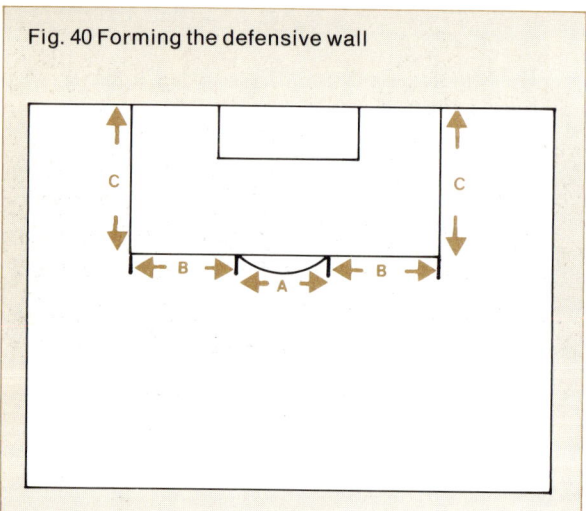

Fig. 40 Forming the defensive wall

When free kicks are awarded against your team in the defensive third a tactical decision has to be made concerning the number of players required to come back into the penalty area. The deciding factor will probably be the position of the kick. For kicks towards the centre of the goal more players are required to form the wall and, therefore, there are fewer players spare to mark opponents and space. In these circumstances every player will probably be withdrawn to bolster the defence, but for free kicks towards the corner flags it may be decided to leave some forward players upfield.

Throw-ins

Without doubt too little attention is paid to throw-ins. This is evident even at the highest level where foul throws are not an uncommon sight. I am always shocked to see top performers infringe the laws of the throw-in, which could not be more simple, (see page 84 **Foul throws**). Each time this happens possession is presented to the opposition and I see no excuse for any youth or senior footballer in this matter. Throw-ins are basically passes and if the throw is for your team the priorities are to retain possession or to strike at goal. If against your side you should combine to make these attacking objectives difficult to succeed. A key factor is concentration, which will enable your team to take throw-ins quickly before the opposition have marked up. Possession should be retained whenever possible so the earlier you are ready to take the throws the greater the chance of finding an unmarked player. Good players pass the ball so that it is easy for the receiver to control the ball. The objectives should be the same with throw-ins and a little consideration before the ball is thrown into play will pay dividends. For example, if the ball is thrown to an unmarked player *do* make sure it goes to feet at a pace that is easy to control and *do not* throw the ball hard so that it bounces up around the waist of the receiver.

The priorities of throw-ins can quickly be summed up in relation to the part of the field that the throw-in is awarded. In the defensive third of the pitch it is vital that we do not lose possession. It is often very difficult to obtain clean possession in this area if the opposition mark tightly. Safety therefore becomes a priority and the ball is safest thrown at an angle of no more than 30 degrees to the line. If possession should be lost defending players are still goal-side of the ball. The most simple ploy is for the receiver to return the ball to the thrower if he should be unmarked. Danger comes when defenders throw the ball square into field which provides little chance of recovery should the ball be lost. These square passes should only be made when there is no danger to the receiver even if his control should let him down.

Often throws made up the line can be used to gain another throw-in farther up the field. If the wide player can draw the defender away from the touch-line the throw can be made between the defender and the touchline so that he has to turn to face his own corner flag. If pressure is exerted and other players mark to deny him the chance of playing back to a supporting player he will be forced to return the ball into touch. Well rehearsed teams can regularly gain ground in this fashion and should the ball be lost they are still in a strong defensive position with players goal-side of the ball.

Middle third

In the middle third of the pitch the dangers of losing possession are not quite so acute because we would have a number of defenders goal-side of the ball. We should, however, remember that the majority of moves leading to goals being scored begin in this section of the field, and also be aware of the danger of square passes that go astray. Therefore, it would be foolish not only to throw away our advantage from an attacking viewpoint, but also from a defensive out-look.

Once again you and your team mates should try to catch your opponents unprepared by an early throw before they have marked up properly. Try to develop the habit of picking the ball up *quickly* so that you can exploit slow marking opponents if the opportunity presents itself.

The most common fault is for players to stand too close to the thrower. This allows no margin of error if the receiver decides to return the ball to the thrower. How many times have you seen possession wasted by an inaccurate return pass going back into touch before he is able to adjust even a few metres. The fact that players stand too close usually also means that a marking opponent can adjust to close down the thrower should the ball be played back to him. You should pull away from the thrower to create

Fig. 41A These players are too close

Fig. 41B Space has now been created

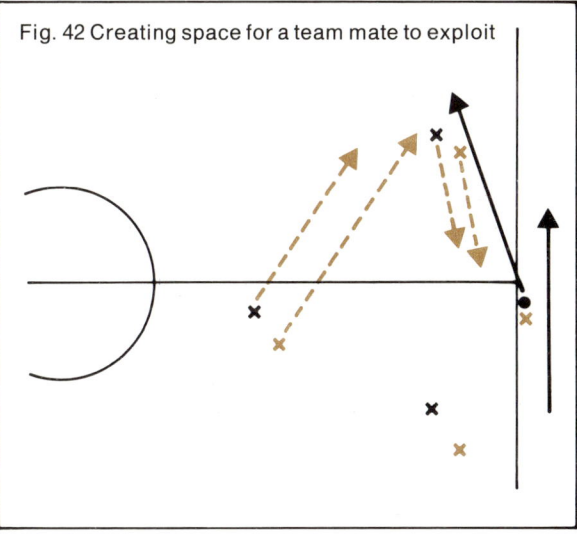

Fig. 42 Creating space for a team mate to exploit

space which gives the thrower time to regain possession and to select his next move (Fig. 41). This space also allows players to time their runs into the space either to a) play a pass back to the thrower b) control the ball themselves in, say, a man to man situation or c) create a space for a team mate to gain possession as in Fig. 42. The principles of attack should be applied to throw-ins where the ultimate aim is *penetration*. Players should always try to go forward, putting as many opposing players as possible on the wrong side of the ball, but only if possession can be retained or the risk of losing possession can be justified by the reward for success.

Attacking third

In this area a gamble can be taken for you should be looking to exert pressure on to the defence by moving the ball into an area where a shot or header for goal is possible. Many players are capable of throwing the ball into the goalmouth, which will always cause defenders concern. I prefer to see throws with a low trajectory to the near post than high looping balls.

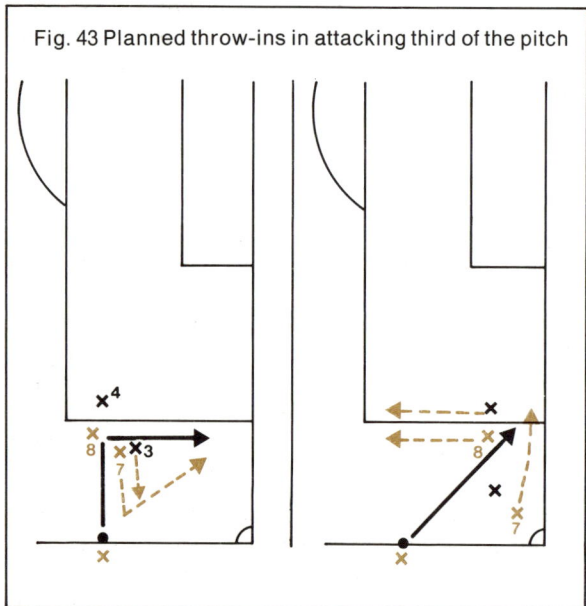

Fig. 43 Planned throw-ins in attacking third of the pitch

If your team does not include a player with this throwing ability one or two planned moves may be the answer. The nearer to goal the attack moves, the tighter the marking becomes and also the space for players to exploit is reduced. Therefore, when a quick throw to maintain possession is not possible players need to create enough space for themselves to play the ball into the goalmouth. Well-planned moves can create space, but co-ordination between the thrower and his team mates is essential. Space can often be made by sudden movement with the ball thrown at precisely the right moment. I have shown two such moves, which are mainly to emphasise the importance of movement.

In Fig. 43A, X7 and X8 stand side by side with their markers on the edge of the penalty area. X7 suddenly darts forward as if to receive the ball, but instead the thrower throws the ball past him to X8, who plays the ball first time towards the goal-line for X7 to turn and collect in a good position. Often his marker X3 loses his man by being distracted when the ball is thrown past him to X8 and is unaware of the danger until it is too late.

In Fig. 43B, X8 stands in a position on the goal-line with X7 near to the corner flag. X8 suddenly sprints along the penalty area calling for the ball and taking his marker with him, leaving a space for X7 to exploit. The thrower should disguise his intention for as long as possible and make sure that X7 can easily control or cross the ball.

Foul throws

I would like to emphasise my concern at the number of foul throws seen at all levels of play, particularly in youth and junior football. You should resolve never to be guilty of this failing and should remember the following causes:

1 Complete lack of concentration – in other words players do not think

Fig. 44A Foot farther away from line is kept forward

Fig. 44B Feet on or behind line; two handed throw

2   Trying to put the ball into play too quickly so that the law is infringed, usually by stepping over the line or lifting a foot from the ground

3   Players standing too close to the thrower so that the ball is dropped rather than thrown in.

Many players place one foot farther up the line than the other when taking a throw-in. This presents no problem as long as it is the foot farther away from the line, because this enables the player to swivel easily to face left or right (Fig. 44). Many players place the inside foot up the line and then have great difficulty if they change their minds and wish to throw backwards rather than upfield. This often leads to a foul throw as the ball is difficult to throw in correctly from the resulting position.

Defending at throw-ins

In the middle, or attacking, thirds of the field we should try to make it very difficult for our opponents to maintain possession. This requires players to be alert because our opponents will be looking to exploit any lack in concentration. Defending is the combined responsibility of players and it requires only one player to neglect to mark his opponent for the efforts of others to be wasted. With good marking, our opponents, not having an easy chance of maintaining possession, will be forced to play for safety, giving us a chance of winning possession.

We have seen earlier that players often return the ball to the thrower. All other players may be marked, but should the thrower be unattended it is not difficult for him to throw the ball accurately for a marked player to return the pass with a simple single touch of the ball. We should, therefore, be alive to the possibility of marking the thrower, thereby denying this most simple way of keeping possession. This can only be achieved if all the other opponents within throwing distance have been marked, for it would be stupidity for a player to mark the thrower, leaving another unmarked player to receive the ball.

85

In the defensive third of the pitch marking is even more vital and players should also try to anticipate the ploys of the opposition. Today, almost every team contains a player with the ability to throw the ball into the goal area and we should be prepared to deal with such dangerous tactics. The higher the ball is thrown, the greater chance we have of adjusting positions, enabling us to compete to head the ball. Our goalkeeper should be prepared to decide if he should challenge for this type of throw, catching or punching the ball above the heads of the other players. When a powerful, head-high throw-in is played accurately towards a forward positioned at the near post, there is little that the goal-side marker can do and the goalkeeper has no time to move to present a challenge. This type of throw-in causes real concern as everything happens so quickly and many goals result from deflections across the face of the goal.

Whenever there is a possibility of the opposition using a throw of this type a defender should be positioned near to the corner of the goal-area, in front of attackers, who should be marked on the goal-side in the usual way. This defender will be able to provide extra competition for the ball and may force the opposition to use a higher throw, thus giving the defenders a better chance of success, making it more difficult for the attackers to head across the face of the goal (Fig. 45).

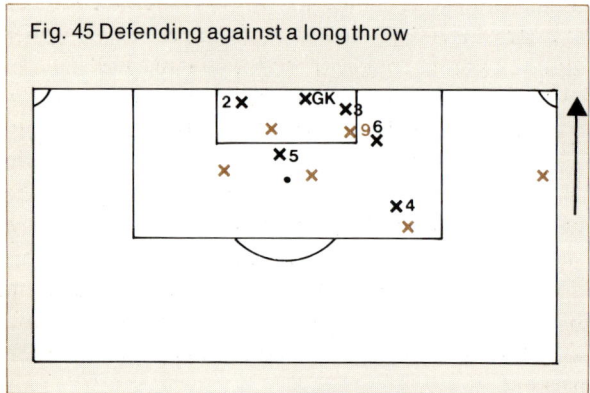

Fig. 45 Defending against a long throw

Corners

To spectators the main attraction of Association Football is in the excitement created in and around the goalmouth. Whenever a team wins a corner kick the air is filled with anticipation because the attackers have the chance of exerting pressure on to the defence in an area from which goals are often scored. Many of the attacking and defensive features are exactly the same for corners as the priorities we have already discussed with free kicks and throw-ins, but we should explore some relevant issues.

To me one thing is perfectly clear. The objective must be to play the ball into a position from where a successful challenge can result in a goal being scored and any corner that fails to achieve this objective is a frivolous waste. The anticlimax created by a corner kick that, for instance, is played directly behind the goal, for a goal kick, can have a derogatory effect on the morale of the players. This is particularly so if the team has had to work hard to achieve the corner and central defenders have moved forward with the hope of capitalising on a rare chance.

Strategy will no doubt be dictated by the strengths and weaknesses of the players playing for and against your team. If your side contains good headers of the ball the objective will be to provide good service with accurate crosses in the air. When the opposition has the stronger player in this department it may be wise to vary the corners by perhaps attacking the near post with a driven ball. The permutations are immense and it requires you and your team mates to give some thought on how best to compete with the opponents of the day.

In crowded penalty areas the movement of players, particularly the goalkeeper, is restricted and it is impossible to pick out any particular player. Therefore, the corners should be aimed at certain priority areas where your colleagues should endeavour to arrive at the right time. Corners should not arrive in the centre of the goal-area because good goalkeepers will only make rare mistakes in gathering this comparatively simple ball. Corners to the near and far posts requiring more difficult decisions by the goalkeeper will pay dividends more frequently.

Corners that bend in flight are more difficult for the goalkeeper to assess. Inswinging corners that curl inside the near or far post are difficult for him to cope with, particularly when challenging players place him under further pressure. Players should practise sending kicks from the corner flag directly into goal, close to the posts and preferably just below the crossbar. Crosses that are bent away from goal have the advantage of coming towards the attackers allowing more power to be exerted into the header or shot.

Points to remember

1   Quality of contact: think about where the corner is to arrive; place the ball to tee it up and concentrate

2   Areas to aim at: near and far posts in areas where goalkeepers have difficulty in using the advantage of their hands

3   The value of swerving kicks

4   If the ball arrives in the chosen areas make sure an attacker makes a challenge

5   Short corners – good variation as long as the ball is eventually played into danger areas

6   Try to 'box' the defence in by using supporting players who can pounce on clearances around the penalty area

7   Take shooting responsibility – in crowded areas where there is not much time to shoot

8   Look for knockdowns and rebounds, where the quickest and bravest forwards score an apparently simple goal.

Defending at corners

When organising our defence at corners we must recognise the most vulnerable areas so that we can mark space as well as players. Any area that the goalkeeper has difficulty in reaching and from where a direct contact can score, is critical. Corners that are floated across spend more time in the air than low crosses and, therefore, allow the goalkeeper more chance to attack the ball. That is why I like to see a defender positioned towards the corner of the goal-area from where he can challenge for any ball of head height or below. This gives the goalkeeper some security if he knows the chosen player will compete for any low corner and he may force the ball to be given more air.

The same object can be achieved by placing a player 10 metres from the kicker, who should adjust his position to move into the line of the kick. This line will vary slightly, depending on whether the kick is an intended inswinger or outswinger, but in any event, it will cause some concern to the kicker, who will probably have to give more height to the corner. This same player will also be able to threaten any short corner that is played.

In the past it was commonplace to position two defenders on the goal-line covering each of the areas inside the posts. I have always agreed with this procedure, but I have noticed that many teams now only use one player on the goal-line and he is positioned at the post nearer to the side where the corner is being taken. I believe this is a mistake as I have seen many goals scored that could have been prevented by such a covering defender. Traditionally it has been the responsibility of the full backs to cover the posts, but it is wasteful to use the talents of a competitive marker who is useful in the air when perhaps a smaller midfield player could do the job equally well.

The priority for other defenders is to mark the spaces which are difficult for the goalkeeper to attack. Those best in the air should cover the areas outside the goal-area to the centre and back of the goal. The goalkeeper must not be restricted by too many people standing in the goal-area. If attackers move into this area too many defenders should not be drawn in with them as this will add to the congestion. Instead, they should cover the areas on the edge of the goal-area.

Chapter 9 Goalkeeping

When I graduated into League Football, it was the high standard of goalkeeping that impressed me most.

I remember my First Division debut for Fulham at Bolton, when twice I thought that I had scored my first league goal, but the agile Wanderers' goalkeeper thwarted me both times. During the next few matches I began to wonder if I would ever prove my scoring ability because shots that were previously rewarded by a goal, were not only saved but often held by the goalkeeper. These goalkeepers made few unforced errors, they anticipated and had such command of the penalty area, that the number of scoring opportunities was greatly reduced. I was left in no doubt about their contribution to the team's success.

The better goalkeepers in schools and in junior football impress mostly with their shot saving abilities. But this is only a fraction of the goalkeeper's responsibility and to do justice to this individual skill I would need to write a whole book on the subject. Instead I will confine myself to a brief outline of the responsibilities and skills involved and recommend to you Ray Clemence's book *Clemence on Goalkeeping* published by Lutterworth Press, for further inspiration.

Fielding the ball

Goalkeepers should act in a similar way to a 'sweeper', constantly assessing play, thereby being prepared to deal with any ball that comes through the defence. Concentration is vital because after long periods of inactivity you may be required to make an important decision. Eighty per cent of the work is gathering the ball without being under a serious challenge. When fielding the ball move your body behind the ball and watch the ball closely – a moment's lapse in concentration can give a goal away – even when no apparent danger exists.

Dealing with an advancing forward

Occasions frequently occur when the goalkeeper must deal with a forward who has broken clear of the defence. There will be times when he needs to leave the penalty area to kick the ball away from an oncoming forward. If the forward is under severe pressure from a defender it may be unwise to advance too far from goal, but if this is not the case it is important that the forward's shooting angle is reduced. This will be achieved by advancing from the goal-line towards the ball. This ground should be made up quickly while the ball is out of the forward's playing distance.

1   *Don't rush* towards him while he is able to play the ball because you will be more easily beaten by a dribble or a direct shot
2   *Make* as large a barrier as possible
3   *Don't dive* too soon or sit down in anticipation of a hard shot
4   *Stay* calm – you may be able to detect his intentions
5   *Try* to dictate to the forward where he must shoot – this is achieved by your approach in a similar way to that of the No. 1 defender
6   *Beware* of the danger of leaving your line when the forward is moving onto a bouncing ball inviting him to lob the ball over your head
7   *Remember* the danger is reduced if the ball is on the ground as chipping is a more difficult skill
8   *If* you dive at his feet spread yourself to present as large a barrier as possible.

Dealing with shots

1   *Keep* your eye on the ball in relation to the feet of the forward – this will help in anticipation
2   *Move* off the line to reduce the shooting angle, thereby reducing the size of the target to the forward
3   *Move* your body behind the ball.

An awareness of your position in relation to the goalposts is essential. This becomes a natural instinct, but only after devoting hours to practice. One small point that may help is for you to be aware that a straight line can be drawn through the corners of the penalty area and goal-area to the nearer post. This will assist you when positioning yourself to deal with any threat on goal from the wings.

Dealing with crosses

When dealing with crosses you must decide if you are able to reach the ball. This will be determined by its flight and the obstructions caused by players. If you are in doubt about leaving your line – *don't!*

Practise catching the ball at its highest point so that when it becomes a necessity you have the confidence to perform the skill. The lower the ball drops, the more chance opponents have of playing the ball, so if there is any threat from an opponent attack the ball and catch it at its highest point.

Crosses that are falling near to the crossbar that are dangerous to catch should be turned over the bar. This is most safely achieved by using the hand farther away from the goal-line.

Practice in decision making is necessary because goalkeepers must decide as early as possible if they can gather the ball. This applies equally to fielding the ball and dealing with shots and crosses. When it is decided not to catch the ball it is necessary to make a firm contact to knock the ball away from the danger area. Whether punching or blocking the ball the same principles should be applied as those of any defensive clearance where a pass is not intended:

1   *Height* – to give time to readjust and to avoid the ball being blocked
2   *Distance* – to allow the defence to reform
3   *Width* – safer because angle is more difficult for opponents to score and there is less likelihood of opponents being there.

Many goals are scored through handling errors when dealing with crosses. Sometimes it is due to a fundamental fault in technique, but more often because:

1   The decision to catch the ball was wrong
2   A poor attempt was made to punch the ball away from danger.

This is undoubtedly an area where constant practice is needed.

Ray Clemence's book will guide you in greater detail and he will help you in such things as improving the various throwing and kicking techniques required for distribution, as well as the exercises that will assist you to develop the physical requirements of the goalkeeper. Goalkeepers are required to be strong as well as supple to develop the level of agility that is needed.

I have only scratched the surface of goalkeeping skills. However, if you are a goalkeeper I hope I have made you aware of some of your responsibilities and have encouraged you to seek the knowledge that will make you a better player.

Chapter 10 Clubs, players and managers

The main objectives in writing this book were not only to help young players to know more about the game, thereby improving their performance, but also to give some guidance to those dedicated people who have the responsibility of organising teams, particularly those containing young footballers. This chapter is about the discipline and attitudes required both by players to make the most of their ability, and by clubs to promote standards that are essential in fostering the correct platform from which players can improve.

The standards that are set and demanded by clubs act as a means of motivation to players. Teams that are indisciplined on the field are most often those whose standards are low. I believe that players need and respond to guide-lines set by clubs and that teams where players come and go as they wish, never maintain high playing standards. I have been involved with senior and junior teams at most levels and I know that players perform better within well organised clubs. Even in professional football where clubs have the greatest demands on their players, many teams suffer from disorganisation in the general everyday running of the club, where players are allowed to behave in an unprofessional way. This often concerns matters apparently unconnected with the playing side but in fact this indiscipline can have a very detrimental effect on playing standards.

Professionalism

If professional clubs can act in an amateurish manner, there is no reason why 'amateur' clubs cannot be professional in their standards. I am not going to determine the rules that clubs should set but I would like to highlight areas where problems often occur and where players should be aware of a definite club policy. In my experience one of the major problems is to do with *training* and *team selection*. What should you do when players do not turn up for training and yet expect their place in the team on the Saturday? This situation is further complicated when a talented player misses training without an acceptable reason, but because of his ability he retains his place in the team over a less

gifted player who never misses a training session. In my opinion, where clubs are only able to train on one or two evenings each week, there can never, other than in an emergency, be an acceptable reason for a player not informing the club that he is unable to attend. There should always be a means of contacting a club official and if this has not been done, I believe the player should forfeit his place in the team. The same discipline should be shown if the reason for absence is unacceptable and although the club's playing results may suffer initially the long term effect can only be beneficial. Players of all abilities will soon accept the situation and as long as the decisions are consistent the spirit within the club must improve.

Many situations occur where players find it impossible to attend club training nights because, for instance, their work prevents them. It is a matter for the club to decide if they are prepared to accept the situation. Personally in this particular case, I would be prepared to use the player as long as he trained at other times to achieve the required level of fitness.

Match days

For football clubs *match days* are the most important of all and clubs should set standards that encourage players into the right frame of mind to play. The time players report before a match should be clearly established, with enough time allowed, to ensure that the final build-up to kick off is spent productively. When attending local league matches, it is commonplace to see players arriving a few minutes before kick off with anxious officials and team mates showing their concern. The late arrival triggers a race against time to be ready for the start of the match, disappointment to the substitute and creates a situation where the team's pre-match preparation must suffer.

Club image

I am always impressed by 'amateur' teams who are not only well organised off the field but who obviously care about presenting a *good image* of their clubs. This may be in the form of playing kit or tracksuits or there may be some uniformity of dress on match days which sets them apart from other teams. This need not be too expensive for I am aware that finance plays an all important role in running of clubs but I know that young players will buy such things as club sweaters and will enjoy identifying with their club in this way. How good it is to see a team turning up in plenty of time for the match and all looking smartly turned out. Quite different from the clubs that turn up 10 minutes before kick-off and looking as if they have just been dragged from their beds! If you are responsible for a club you should consider ways and means of building the right spirit so that players are proud of representing their team. This means that considerable thought should be given to the image and administrative organisation so that the name of your club always gains the respect and admiration of opponents and outsiders.

Communication

Earlier I mentioned the importance of the players talking to one another during matches. Many observers may be unconvinced that a football field should be a place where shouting takes place, but I can assure you that it is a valuable asset to a player.

There are numerous occasions during a match where players are unable to see the options that are open and where they rely on a team mate's advice. Players in possession who are pressurised by opponents are often so totally obsessed with keeping the ball that they are unable to lift their head to see unmarked colleagues. In these circumstances a call allows the player to play the ball to a team mate, who might otherwise have been unnoticed. In fact a colleague's voice acts as an additional pair of eyes.

Even when a player on the ball has an opportunity to look for himself he should welcome demands for the ball from team mates. It is always pleasing to know that other players have found good supporting positions and that they want the ball. This is a feature of the play of the better teams, for it is usually the poorer sides whose lack of confidence is illustrated by players not seeking possession of the ball.

It is possible to tell a player how much time he has by merely calling his name. If we imagine a colleague gaining possession of the ball with an opponent moving in to challenge from behind, a quiet call of 'John' will tell him that you are available and that he has plenty of time to execute a pass. If he delays his pass and the opponent begins to close in to threaten him the increasing urgency in your voice, as you call 'John, JOHN, JOHN!' will communicate the increasing pressure that is being exerted on him.

Another example of the voice being so helpful is when an attacker is closing in at an acute angle to goal with the goalkeeper to beat. The chances of scoring would be greater if he passed to an unmarked colleague approaching the middle of the goal. If his colleague calls his name quietly he may ignore the call and shoot for goal – most likely into the side netting. In the same circumstance a demanding call of 'JOHN' would have encouraged the pass to be made for a simple goal to be scored.

There are times when calling is unconstructive, but like all other footballing skills, players must learn when it can be advantageous. I can never understand onlookers who rebuke the concept of communication for team games require players to build understanding in this way.

Standards

Standards both on and off the field are equally important and in fact are usually related. Teams with a responsible attitude off the pitch are usually disciplined on the field of play, whereas clubs who do not set their players standards often have problems during matches. This relates both to the player's individual responsibilities to the team's performance and also to the standard of conduct. Over the last few years cases of misconduct have risen steadily and much of this responsibility must be laid at the feet of those who manage or coach the teams. More can be done to influence players so that they do not become involved in this unhealthy part of the game.

Dissent

Dissent is a contagious disease. A side containing just one player with this tendency, can adversely influence other team mates towards the same deficiency. Such teams then argue over almost every decision that goes against them. It is vital that team organisers firmly discourage such players before the general discipline is destroyed. Remember that:

1 Players respond to clear standards
2 Good clubs set standards of discipline for their players – both on and off the field
3 Good clubs treat offenders objectively – irrespective of ability
4 At any level of play the club is more important than any individual.

Team managers and coaches, particularly of young players, have a tremendous responsibility to encourage the right attitude to the game, at the same time presenting the game in the most enjoyable way possible to develop the ability and character of the players. The manager is the players' direct link with the club and is therefore the person who should ensure that the players abide by the club's rules. If you hold a similar position within a club, I sincerely hope that I have stimulated your enthusiasm even further and have provided one or two ideas which will assist you.

Motivating the team

Coaches and managers work and control their players in various ways but once the match begins there is little that they can do to influence the play. They should, however, endeavour to motivate the team before the match, provide constructive observations and the appropriate tactical changes at half-time and an after-match analysis that provides a basis for an improved performance.

The pre-match build-up is influenced by the knowledge of the players in the team. Each will be motivated in a different way and an important aspect of team management is concerned with understanding the various characteristics of individuals. Some need to be coaxed into believing in their ability whereas others may be stimulated by strong demands for a good performance. Some people have an ability to motivate players through their own personality. You may be one of those lucky people who can bring players into a suitable frame of mind to exploit their talent to the full. Some managers work on the basis of building confidence by playing down the ability of the opponents while at the same time enthusing over the qualities of their own team. This method may be successful for some but for others it only produces a casual performance. Other managers work in the opposite way by making the task seem very difficult in the belief that players will give of their best to match their opponents. Sometimes this has a detrimental effect on some players who find the task ahead too daunting. So you can see that motivating players is an individual technique.

In the final build up before matches, all of us can encourage the players to focus their thoughts on the game ahead. This will enable you to remind the players of their collective and individual responsibilities. Each player could be spoken to individually when your knowledge of their personalities will help you to motivate them. I always feel that it is important to encourage all the members of the team to make contributions by expressing their opinions and making suggestions about the team's methods. This will help even the newest club member to feel part of the team.

At half-time you have an opportunity to make adjustments. You must be careful not to confuse the players by over-complicating matters. I select a few outstanding team problems, as too many items will be difficult to convey within the half-time interval.

The inquest

After matches, I feel that the pattern should be the same whether you have won, drawn or lost. Joining in the elation or disappointment is a part of the game although I have heard of managers who rarely came into the dressing room if the game had been lost! I do not think it advisable to have an inquest of the match immediately you arrive in the dressing room. At the end of a match, players are still under the emotional effects of the game and criticism in these circumstances can often develop into heated situations. A story was told to me many years ago about a boxer who had lost a very close fight on points and on returning to his dressing room was criticised by his trainer. The boxer, still warm and full of disappointment, produced the knockout blow that he had failed to find during the fight! I have always remembered this supposedly true story and agree that there is little point in discussing issues that can be more productive when players have recovered their composure. The trainer's criticism may have been well-founded and had the point been raised the next day when the flow of adrenalin had slowed, the boxer may well have found the opinion constructive and have accepted his viewpoint.

Everyone enjoys receiving praise but none of us like being criticised. Try to marry the two when criticising young players because confidence must be maintained. For the same reasons it is often easier to be critical following a victory for not only can you be harder on individuals without destroying the confidence but it brings teams back down to earth.

Realising your potential

I presume that young players reading this book are keen to become better footballers. If nothing else, I hope that I have stimulated you to think about the game in depth so that your understanding will lead to even greater enjoyment whether you are playing a match or watching. During my career I have worked with teenagers of varying abilities. Many have been professional players but the majority have been involved at other levels. The main factor in determining your level of play is ability and your aim should be to play at the highest level that your ability will allow. That is why this book should be interpreted to the level of your own ability so that you can be one of the better players at your standard of play. Only then can you

hope to progress to a higher level when the challenge to reach the top of that strata starts again.

For players to attain their full potential, there are factors other than ability, which make an important contribution. Your character and your attitude will substantially determine the impact you make. Set yourself standards on and off the field which will allow your potential to be fulfilled. I will discuss some of the factors that I feel are important. Individually they are significant, together they build a picture of yourself.

Reliability

Many people are completely unreliable. There is always a doubt about them turning up to play or train, even though they promise a few hours before to be there. Of course it does not happen every time and when it does they smile their way through an apology, always forgetting that there can never be an excuse for not sending a message through – of course it will never happen again, but invariably it does. *Reliability* is a must. There are people on whom you know you can rely, so be like them and not like those who allow themselves occasional lapses.

Punctuality

Linked to reliability must be *punctuality*. Players who turn up late for training or matches erode the standards of clubs. Times should be set by the club and *you* should be sure to abide by them. Clubs who train once or twice a week need every minute together. It is easy for late arrivals to whittle a two hour session down to little over an hour, by the time they have changed and warmed up. Clubs should beware of this problem that will become worse as the season progresses, if not checked immediately. Travel time to away matches must be calculated so that arrival at the ground allows ample time to change and prepare properly. Late arrivals cause unnecessary concern and diminish time spent in final preparation.

Appearance

Teams should be well turned out when they go onto the field of play. Even if your club cannot afford new kit, there is no excuse for starting the match in dirty playing strip. I am aware that some clubs expect their players to look after their complete strip. Others supply a clean shirt and players bring along their shorts and socks. Whatever the situation, make sure that you are not responsible for contributing to a scruffy turn-out. Standards are important so be sure your kit is clean for every match.

The most important piece of equipment for the footballer is his boots. Dirty boots usually reflect on the attitude of the player. They are an expensive necessity to the footballer and their life can vary depending on how they are cared for. Their life will be extended if they are cleaned immediately after a match, and allowed to dry before being polished.

Teams often arrive in plenty of time for a match but they finish up in a panic to be ready on time. This has invariably been caused by a boot problem that would have been solved had the boots been cleaned and checked. It may be that the laces have snapped or that a screw-in stud has needed changing and then it is discovered that the thread has rusted up. Before each game, players should inspect the pitch to decide the length of stud that should be used. If the studs are not checked and the threads lubricated frequently, a problem could arise when trying to replace a stud and this could cause a serious delay if the stud should snap during the struggle to release it.

Fitness and training

There have been many surveys to ascertain the distance that players cover during the 90 minutes of a match. The results have varied depending on the playing position and the standard of play, but 10 kilometres is accepted as a reasonable figure. In all the reports, a third of the total distance has been calculated as being covered at speed. When the many stops, starts, jumps and falls are considered along with the physical challenges that are made, it is obvious that players need to be fit to satisfy the demands of the game. That is why the player's attitude to *training* must be good.

You must train as hard as you can to reach the fitness level that enables you to attain your full potential. If everybody trains in an identical way with precisely the same dedication, the recorded performances would all vary because physical capabilities vary from person to person. As long as you are giving 100 per cent there is no shame in your performance being inferior to that of a team mate. He may be capable of more, but constantly trains well within his limits, so although he records superior results when performances are tested and measured, he never reaches his potential.

Knowing the laws

It is surprising how ignorant players are about the laws of Association Football. It is in your interest to know them well so do something about it. You can buy a copy of the Referees' Chart or better still apply to your local Football Association for details of qualifying courses for referees or coaches which will help to broaden your knowledge.

Successful players, whether they be young or old, are those with the right attitude towards the game. Success brings added enjoyment and this can only be attained if a team's technical ability can be complemented by a positive attitude. Competition between two teams is the essence of football and often the difference between winning and losing is the attitude that players have towards the match.

Some players are 'competitors' in every sense of the word whereas others seem to lack the determination that allows their talent to blossom. Acquiring this asset is not easy but the first step is to understand the importance of being positive. Perhaps your attitude could be better and it may be restricting you from becoming a better player. Whatever level of development you have attained, these sentiments from a well-known poem may help you to become a better player:

Life's battles don't always go to the stronger or faster man
For sooner or later the man who wins is the man who thinks he can.

Index